Frank E. Frothingham

The Boston Fire

Its History together with the Losses in Detail of both Real and Personal

Estate

Frank E. Frothingham

The Boston Fire

Its History together with the Losses in Detail of both Real and Personal Estate

ISBN/EAN: 9783337253295

Printed in Europe, USA, Canada, Australia, Japan

Cover: Foto ©ninafisch / pixelio.de

More available books at **www.hansebooks.com**

THE BOSTON FIRE.

THE BOSTON FIRE,

November 9th and 10th, 1872.

ITS HISTORY,

TOGETHER WITH THE LOSSES IN DETAIL OF BOTH REAL AND PERSONAL ESTATE. ALSO, A COMPLETE
LIST OF INSURANCE LOSSES,

AND

AN APPENDIX

CONTAINING THE CITY LOAN, INSURANCE, AND BUILDING ACTS,

BY

F. E. FROTHINGHAM,
Recently of the Assessors' Department.

BOSTON:
LEE & SHEPARD, PUBLISHERS.
NEW YORK:
LEE, SHEPARD & DILLINGHAM.
1873.

Entered, according to Act of Congress, in the year 1873, by
F. E. FROTHINGHAM,
In the Office of the Librarian of Congress, at Washington.

PRINTED AT
𝕿𝖍𝖊 𝕮𝖍𝖚𝖗𝖈𝖍 𝕻𝖗𝖊𝖘𝖘,
HARTFORD, CONN.

THE BOSTON FIRE.

There is a section of Boston lying south and east of State and Washington streets, and north of Summer street, which was once the home of her merchant princes, but which has been invaded by the onward march of trade. At the time of the calamity, the story of which we are about to relate, almost the entire territory within the lines mentioned was covered with palatial warehouses, built of granite, brick, and iron. The aristocratic mansions had been demolished, and in their places had risen magnificent palaces of trade, until every street in the district was flanked by the most substantial and architecturally beautiful edifices on this continent, if not in the world.

In those lofty structures which graced Franklin, Summer, High, Pearl, Federal, Congress, and Devonshire streets, were piled up the accumulated products of Lowell, Lawrence, Manchester, Lewiston, and other milling places, as well as the results of the labor of toiling thousands in the boot and shoe manufactories throughout the eastern portion of Massachusetts. Here, too, was centred nearly all the large clothing establishments, in which thousands of females found employment; the entire stock of wool within the domain of

Boston was stored there; several of the largest printing establishments, crockery warehouses, and iron and wholesale furnishing and fancy goods stores were located in this district.

Such was the section of the city of which we write, on the afternoon of the 9th of November, 1872, when seven hundred places of business within the black lines of the map were closed by the proprietors, who retired to their homes with the fullest confidence in the security of their possessions against fire and robbery.

The Fire Department of Boston had long been a source of pride to its citizens, and challenged competition with any city in America, officered as it was by men whose long experience, cool judgment, and daring had met every exigency that years of municipal growth and commercial prosperity required of them. A single but temporary defect existed in the department, occasioned by the prevalence of an epizootic influenza among the horses, which for several weeks had incapacitated this important branch of the department in the performance of their labors. While this fact was acknowledged as a defect, security was felt from the prompt and well-devised means which the Board had improvised. But an emergency seldom found in the known history of the world was before them. The alarm-bell from the now historic box, 52, signalled a fire, which was discovered almost instantly at every window of the large four-story granite building, with a French roof, situated at the corner of Summer and Kingston streets. The dread alarm of the tocsin was sounded throughout the city, and was repeated a second, third, and fourth time, summoning to the scene the entire Fire Department. The origin of the fire will ever remain a mystery, but from the best evidence that can be obtained, it resulted in some way from the fires of the furnaces which lay beneath the boilers in the basement, to heat the block with steam. Before the firemen were able to combat the flames, the fire had obtained complete mastery of the building, the interior of which being destroyed, the walls fell outward, spreading inflammable matter in every direction; but, before the walls crumbled, the elastic flame, feeding upon the light materials of which the modern Mansard roofs were constructed, leaped across Summer street, and spread with remorseless fury from block to block, with a rapidity which baffled the exertions of their most determined opponents. Gathering heat and force at every point, and forcing back the determined firemen and the crowds of spectators who had by this time assembled, the fire worked its way in the face of the wind, which was from a northerly direction, toward the wealthiest portion of this section. One after another the massive blocks crumbled and fell, and before midnight the flames had enveloped Winthrop square, both sides of Summer street below Trinity Church, and the buildings between Summer and Franklin streets, and rushing down Devonshire street to within a few doors of Milk street, had converted the long rows of granite and freestone palaces of trade into red and roaring seas of flame. Dismayed, but still undaunted, the heroic firemen fought the common enemy. Realizing the inability of his own force to cope with so formidable an adversary, the chief of the department despatched messages over the electric wires, summoning assistance from the departments of other cities; and from the towns in the immediate vicinity of Boston, and places more remote, firemen hastened with alacrity, some hauling their engines by hand, some by horses, and others brought in by railroads. At half-past ten o'clock the fire had made such progress, that one who made the circuit of the flames at that hour, was compelled to pass through Bedford, High, Congress, and Franklin streets. Sparks, driven by the wind, flew through these streets with the thickness of a snow-squall, and large flakes of burning wood were carried by the wind down into the bay and over the south shore. Some of them fell on the light wooden structure of the Hartford and Erie depot, and set that on fire, and the flames of this communicating with the coal-sheds and offices on the harbor front, found material to feed their progress on the eastern side of Broad street. Before midnight, the great thoroughfares of trade before mentioned, hedged in by a wealth of unique architecture, the broad show-windows of which were rich with the arrays of the products of the loom, had been swept by the fiery element. All had vanished from view, and one broad plane of ruin, dotted here and there by a crumbling column or tottering wall, marked the spot of their former grandeur. Powerless to stem the torrent of flame which threatened to extend its devastating hand across Washington and State streets, and sweep away all the old historic piles of the ancient city, the firemen retreated. A huge mass of flame arose from the acres of burning buildings, illuminating every tower and steeple, and reflecting itself upon the heavens, so that its lurid glare could be seen for a hundred miles.

The alarm spread in every direction, and at midnight the

streets were filled with people of all classes and conditions, who hurried hither and thither, with bundles of goods snatched from the fire. They came from every direction; great and excited crowds of humanity, whose interest in the terrible scene arose not from an idle or speculative curiosity, but the more potent considerations of personal interest. Merchants hurried to their safes, from which they removed their most valuable possessions; clerks rushed to the stores of their employers, and carried away goods; truckmen and teamsters harnessed their horses, and galloped them to the scene of devastation, reaping a harvest from their old patrons, whose stocks they removed.

And still the flames spread with ever-increasing intensity. Iron shutters were warped and melted; granite columns crumbled and fell; while the great piles of cotton and woollen fabrics furnished fuel for the fire, which gleamed with a horrid glare, engulfing everything combustible in the general ruin. The entire block bounded by Summer, Otis, and Devonshire streets, and Winthrop square, was consumed, and the fire, leaping across Franklin street, and breaking through the rear walls of the great jobbing houses, attacked similar structures on Devonshire street, which fell a prey to the devouring element. The flames poured forth from the stores on both sides of Federal street, and meeting, converted that thoroughfare into a solid mass of roaring fire. The long and substantial blocks ranged on either side of Congress, Pearl, High, and Purchase streets, were seized upon and consumed with the speed of a whirlwind. Revelling in its destruction, and creating a storm of smoke and ashes, in which no man could breathe, the fire made terrible way toward Washington and Milk streets, and strode onward toward the harbor. As the great torrent of flame spread over the doomed territory, a deep and sullen boom broke upon the midnight air. The entire blocks of buildings facing on both sides of Federal street, some sixty in number, were blown up in the vain hope of arresting the flames. A similar course was pursued with the buildings on Congress, between Milk and Water streets, in rear of the new post-office, which stately edifice stood like adamant in the path of the flames. The struggle to prevent the fire from crossing Washington street was severe. All the way from Summer down to Milk street, the firemen fought the enemy inch by inch, amid falling walls and intense heat. As the walls fell, burying several of the heroic men, their comrades retreated, but kept pouring streams of water incessantly upon the buildings on the west side of the street, thereby lessening a calamity, the extent of which would have been appalling to think of. But the fire turned its face toward Milk street, threatening the Old South Church, upon the fate of which hinged the destiny of all that portion of the city between it and State street. The extinction of the flames on the south side of Milk street prevented the expansion of the disaster, while the new post-office building forced the flames to make a detour through Congress and Water streets. At daybreak on Sunday morning the fire was completely encircled by a line of engines, manned by brave men, whose lives were constantly endangered, but who fought a gallant and winning fight at every point. The fire was then fully under control on its southern line, and extended only a few numbers from Summer street on Chauncy, Kingston,

Lincoln, South, and Bedford streets; but on the harbor front it had swept everything before it, from the junction of Summer and Federal streets nearly to Oliver street. Liberty square was in ruins, and before noon the fire had seized upon the old post-office and sub-treasury in Merchants' Exchange building, compelling a removal of the deposits to the Custom-house, and mails to the "Cradle of Liberty"—Faneuil Hall. At noon on Sunday the fire was under control at every point, and that night many of the steam fire engines from out of town were dismissed, and returned to their homes. But the weary firemen were destined to renewed exertions, from a source least to be expected, for about one o'clock on Monday morning several explosions of gas occurred in the Summer street sewer, setting fire to the extensive jewelry store at the corner of Washington street. The fire spread with great rapidity, but through the heroic energy and greater skill of the firemen, the flames were soon conquered, not, however, till several stores had been destroyed. Such, in general terms, was the memorable conflagration of the 9th and 10th of November, which swept over the wealthiest business portion of the city, destroying, in addition to the buildings devoted to trade, Trinity Church on Summer street, St. Stephen's Church on Purchase street, the Boston, Hartford and Erie Railroad Depot, six banks, a number of stereotype founderies, newspaper and printing offices, including the "Transcript," "Pilot," "Saturday Evening Gazette," "Waverley Magazine," the State printing establishment. The small freighting schooner, Louisa Frazer, was burned at her wharf on Broad street. More of the shipping would have been destroyed but for the work of the steam tugs, which were vigorously used in towing them into the stream, out of reach of the flames.

The injury to the business of Boston is far greater than the computations made upon the goods and buildings destroyed, and it cannot be given in dollars and cents. In the preceding paragraph the estates other than those devoted to the trades were specified, but in summing up the extent of the disaster to the business community, it is in order to refer more particularly to the stores and warehouses. The entire space occupied by the wholesale dry goods dealers, wool merchants, boot and shoe, and hide and leather dealers, and clothing houses was of that swept over. Not a wool house was left standing in the city. Every wholesale clothing house in Boston, with a single exception, and the wholesale boot and shoe houses, or all but one, were laid in ruins, and but three or four dry goods commission houses were left standing. The amount of foreign, domestic, fleece and pulled wool destroyed by the fire cannot fall short of 8,000,000 pounds, while the entire stock remaining in the market consisted of foreign wool, and is less than 8,000 bales. The destruction of boots, shoes, and leather was quite as complete as that of wool, although the stock of leather goods in warehouses was much lighter than it would have been a month later, and the loss was, consequently, much less to the owners.

In addition to the firemen who came with their engines from the towns and cities immediately surrounding Boston, steamers came from Norwich and New Haven, Connecticut; Portland and Biddeford, Maine; Portsmouth and Manchester, New Hampshire; Salem, Lynn, Newburyport, Lawrence, Worcester, Fall River, Taunton, and New Bedford; and offers of assistance were at once received from all quarters.

During the progress of the fire, multitudes of people flocked to the scene, rendering it necessary to employ the entire force of the police to prevent the people from rushing into the burning district, and embarrassing the firemen in their operations. Even this proved insufficient, and the Mayor of the city having applied for military assistance to the Governor of the State, the following responded to the call : First Regiment of Infantry, First and Second Battalions of Infantry, Independent Cadets, First Battalion of Cavalry, while United States troops, from the forts in the harbor, and the Ninth Regiment M. V. M. subsequently reported for duty. A guard was maintained over the district for over two weeks.

So great was the interest felt in the fate of the city, that the people, instead of attending Divine service, thronged the streets immediately about the fire, and churches were deserted for miles around; and extra trains on the steam railroads brought thousands of people to the city. Thieves were plentiful enough in Boston at the outbreak, but as the telegraph told the story of the conflagration in other large cities, the leeches upon the public body in human form hastened to the scene, with visions of immense plunder. Chief Savage had prepared for this most admirably. At the earliest moment he redistricted the city, and hundreds of "specials" were instructed in the duties devolving upon the police. One of the chief difficulties the police had to deal with was the free delivery of goods to the masses by the owners of the stores on fire. As it was, the amount collected and taken to the station-houses was found to aggregate $80,000 in value, and during Saturday night and Sunday morning, four hundred and sixty persons were arrested.

While the flames were yet in progress, a large body of citizens convened at the Mayor's office, in the City Hall, and coöperated with the City Government in such action as was necessary, in view of the great calamity. The emergency developed the best energies and sentiments of the community.

The immediate work was to relieve the distressed, to encourage the desponding, and take advanced steps toward rebuilding the district. Generous offers of aid poured in from all over the country, while large supplies of bread, meat, coffee, and soup were distributed to the firemen at their posts of labor. Chicago, which, eleven months before, to a day, had passed through the same trying ordeal, with a promptness and liberality beyond all praise, through the action of her Mayor and citizens, sent a committee to Boston with $100,000. This action was heralded by the following messages:

MAYOR'S OFFICE, CHICAGO,
November 10, 1872.

To the Mayor of Boston:

The citizens of Chicago tender their deepest sympathy and all the material aid in their power to your afflicted people in this hour of their misfortune. In what way can we help you most? I have called a public meeting for to-morrow, to consider ways and means of assistance.

JOSEPH MEDILL,
Mayor.

CHICAGO,
November 10, 1872.

To the Hon. Wm. Gray:

Our people desire to do everything possible for a city that came so nobly to our aid as Boston did. Tell me what we can do. We will share with you whatever we have left.

WIRT DEXTER,
Chairman Ex. Com., Chicago R. & M. Society.

The Boston City Council adopted resolutions expressive of its sympathy for the sufferers by the fire, and appointed a committee for the purpose of extending immediate aid to those needing assistance, and also tendered a vote of thanks to the firemen.

In this connection it is proper to state, that although but few people were rendered houseless by the conflagration, yet at least twenty thousand shop girls and other persons were thrown out of employment. A relief bureau was established, and contributions of money and clothing, as well as offers of employment, were received.

The most distressing feature of the calamity was the loss of life, the extent of which will probably never be satisfactorily ascertained; while hundreds were more or less injured by the falling of walls, beneath which all of thirty people were killed. The following are the names of persons known or believed to be buried in the ruins: Franklin Olmstead, of Cambridge, killed; Wm. S. Frazier, of Cambridge Port, killed; Walter S. Twombly, of Maplewood, killed; Lewis C. Thompson, of Worcester, killed; Geo. W. Hunkins, of Amesbury, missing; Michael Fitzgerald, of East Boston, missing; William Fitzgerald, of South Boston, killed; Martin Gallagher, city laborer, killed; John Dillon, of

South Boston, killed; John Connolly, of West Roxbury, killed; Geo. W. Tuck, of Haverhill, missing; Henry Weston, of Utica, New York, missing; Henry Rogers, of Boston, killed; Daniel Cochrane, of Boston, killed; Captain William Farry, of Boston, killed; George N. Pullen, of Boston, missing; Mrs. Coleman and two children, of Boston, killed; James Crawford, of East Milton, missing; Robert Williams, of Boston, missing; Frank McKee, of Boston, killed; John Hughes, of Milford, missing; Andrew Thacherty, John H. Chase, Geo. Bach, Edwin Beal, and Michael Cuddy—all missing.

[Doubtless there are others than those named who are of the killed and missing and, further, that nearly all here classified as missing, will be eventually believed among the killed.—ED.]

The calamity swept out of existence millions of property, impoverished hundreds of business men, and broke all but two of the local insurance companies of the city. But the merchants of Boston have still left to them their fortitude, energy, and business capacity, which speedily manifested itself in their determination to rise above the depressing influences of the occasion, and applied themselves at once to the work of reconstruction. Before the fire had ceased burning, and while everything was unsettled, a large number of merchants secured new quarters, and resumed business on Monday morning. Others commenced the erection of temporary buildings, some on the ruins of their warehouses, and on the site of Fort hill. Washington square, in this locality, was soon covered with buildings of corrugated iron, and occupied by boot, shoe, leather, and iron dealers. The dispersion of trade carried the various branches of business into strange localities. The dining-rooms of hotels were transformed into dry goods stores and tailoring establishments. West India goods, and cases of boots and shoes, encumbered the same sidewalks. One large boot and shoe house went north, to Canal street; a lace and embroidery dealer moved south, to Dover street; and every vacant store within a circuit of a mile was let at a large advance upon the regular rentals, with enormous bonuses as primary considerations.

During the three weeks succeeding the fire, the ruins were visited by tens of thousands of people daily, who gazed at the sad reality, and contemplated the situation, while all around them the busy gangs of men laid low the dangerous walls, worked upon the safes, or sought the remains of friends.

THE FOLLOWING

DETAILS OF LOSSES, BY STREETS,

WERE TAKEN FROM

The Assessors' Books of 1872.

DETAILS OF LOSSES BY STREETS.

ARCH STREET.

Names.	Nos.	Value of Land.	Value of Buildings.	Square Feet of Land.	Personal.
President and Fellows, Harvard College	1–3	$75,000	$25,000	5,300	....
Geo. S. Winslow & Co.	5	....	....	....	$112,800
Whittemore, Cabot & Co.	5	....	....	....	30,000
Mortimer C. Feris	11–15	18,000	10,000	1,300	....
Fernald & Co.	....	....	....	....	15,000
A. F. Wheaton & Co.	....	....	....	....	3,000
Ed. M. Winslow	6	17,000	19,000	1,350	20,000
Boone, Cannell & Co.	....	....	....	....	1,000
C. B. Grinnell	8	....	....	....	1,000
J. & J. F. Lee	10–12	13,000	12,000	1,030	....
Matthew Binney's Sons	14–16	13,000	12,000	1,015	....
W. P. Brigham & Co.	"	....	....	....	6,000
J. B. Babcock, J. W. Partridge	"	....	....	....	3,000

BATH STREET.

Names.	Nos.	Value of Land.	Value of Buildings.	Square Feet of Land.	Personal.
James Vila (heirs)	1	$28,000	$12,000	2,500	....
Walmouth Manufacturing Co.	....	....	....	....	$8,300
J. Lawrence et als. (trustees)	5	23,000	7,000	2,000	....
Mead & Addy	....	....	....	....	5,000
D. E. Fitzgerald	....	....	....	....	2,000

BROAD STREET.

Names.	Nos.	Value of Land.	Value of Buildings.	Square Feet of Land.	Personal.
E. P. Dolbeare (heirs)	258	$19,000	$1,000	14,000	....
E. P. Dolbeare & Co.	....	....	....	....	$1,000
Lewis & Scott	....	....	....	....	600
Prescott & Chapin	270	120,000	8,000	50,000	20,000
Brewer & Wheeler	282	....	....	....	2,500
Liverpool Wharf Co.	....	80,000	3,000	40,000	....
J. J. & M. F. Fenelon	....	....	....	....	1,000
H. B. Inches et als.	398	210,000	30,000	85,536	25,000
Pendle'on & Rose	....	....	....	....	1,500
J. Vaughan & Co.	....	....	....	....	2,600
Allison & Mason	....	....	....	....	2,500
Hodgkins & Blodgett	....	....	....	....	65,000
T. Remick	....	160,000	5,000	80,000	....
W. H. Prentis (heirs)	324	....	....	....	800
B. Mansfield	....	....	....	....	15,000
W. H. Prentis & Son	....	108,000	2,000	45,000	....
T. Tileston (heirs)	346	....	....	....	8,000
J. & W. Stewart	....	110,000	10,000	45,000	....
B. H. & Erie R. R.	....	....	....	....	500
Frost & Davis	....	14,000	1,000	2,496	....
Leonard Ware	299	....	....	....	45,000
Thompson & Wilson	....	7,000	5,000	1,222	....
L. Ware	307	....	....	....	40,000
G. Lawton & Co.	....	7,000	5,000	1,223	....
L. Ware	311				

DETAILS OF LOSSES.

Name	No.			
L. Ware & Sons	......	......	......	37,000
A. & J. Tirrell	351	16,000	1,955	......
R. Bishop	......	......	......	5,000
F. C. Carruth (heirs)	353	19,000	2,931	......
Hill & Cutler	......	......	......	14,000
R. G. Norris	363	20,000	2,606	......
L. Parks (heirs)	......	12,000	1,650	......
F. P. Preston	......	......	......	500
A. Emerson & Co	......	......	......	12,000
L. Parks	379	12,000	1,650	......
"	383	12,000	1,650	......
"	387	12,000	1,650	......
"	383	......	......	......
Porter & Co	......	......	......	7,000
Bent, Crane & Co	......	......	......	15,000
L. Larkin	393	20,000	2,586	......
J. & A. Tirrell	397	16,000	2,201	......
S. B. Morse	401	11,000	1,443	......
D. Chamberlain	403	11,000	1,460	......
Titcomb & Timson	......	......	......	15,000
Mary Tileston (heirs)	411	44,000	4,860	......

BUSSEY PLACE.

Name	No.				
J. Ingersoll Bowditch	9	$6,000	$4,500	1,365	......
Wendell Phillips	7	6,000	4,500	1,325	......
Samuel G. Reed	5	7,500	6,500	1,325	......
Mortimer C. Ferris	3	11,000	5,000	1,330	......
J. Farwell, Jr., & Co	......	......	......	......	$5,000

CHANNING STREET.

Names.	Nos.	Value of Land.	Value of Buildings.	Square Feet of Land.	Personal.
Geo. Parkman (heirs)	13	$11,000	$3,000	1,027	......
"	15	10,000	3,000	1,363	......
J. B. Glover	6–8	11,000	5,000	1,520	......
G. F. Moore & Co.	......	......	......	......	$10,000

COLUMBIA STREET.

Names.	Nos.	Value of Land.	Value of Buildings.	Square Feet of Land.	Personal.
Henry Lee	89	$20,000	$3,000	1,339	......
"	91	13,000	2,500	1,367	......
"	95	11,000	3,000	1,203	......
"	97	11,000	3,000	1,223	......
"	99	13,000	3,000	1,328	......
"	101	13,000	4,000	1,000	......
"	103	19,000	6,000	1,100	......

CONGRESS STREET.

Names.	Nos.	Value of Land.	Value of Buildings.	Square Feet of Land.	Personal.
John Fleet (heirs)	98–110	$28,000	$12,000	2,438	......
F. Upton & Co	......	......	......	......	$75,000
G. A. Kramer	110	35,000	20,000	3,650	......
"	112	14,000	8,000	1,392	......
J. W. Fenno (heirs)	120	12,000	8,000	1,060	......

DETAILS OF LOSSES.

A. M. Nelson & Co.					3,500
Kensington & Sawyer					3,000
D. Whitemore					30,000
A. J. Morse	124	30,000	27,000	3,600	20,200
" & Son	130	31,000	31,000	4,935	275,000
J. Lawrence et als. (trustees)					
Morse, Denny & Co.	136	31,000	31,000	4,830	30,000
George Blackburn (heirs)					83,200
Lockwood & Clark					
G. Blackburn & Co.	148	30,000	25,000	4,100	2,000
M. Williams					35,000
N. P. Hallowell					
J. L. & H. C. Rogers	154	30,000	30,000	4,400	50,000
F. Allen (heirs)					12,000
J. R. Nichols & Co.	162	30,000	30,000	4,366	115,000
C. C. Priest & Co.					
F. S. Carruth (heirs)	165	25,000	25,000	3,200	200 000
Clark, Adams & Clark	174	45,000	35,000	5,646	160,000
J. S. Potter					165,900
Baily & Jenkins	176–182	43,000	17,000	5,960	250,000
W. B. Spooner					5,000
Johnson, Eaton & Brackett	184	16,000	11,000	2,337	81,900
Harding, Gray & Devoy					
Johnson & Thompson	190–192	27,000	20,000	3,392	40,000
A. Thompson & Co.					
Abbott & Fernald					
E. B. Phillips					
" & Co.					
E. B. Phillips					
J. & H. K. Osborn					

CONGRESS STREET—*Continued.*

Names.	Nos.	Value of Land.	Value of Buildings.	Square Feet of Land.	Personal.
J. O. Safford	196–198	$20,000	$14,000	2,646	......
" " & Co	......	......	......	......	$75,000
J. Tuttle	212–216	52,000	40,000	6,669	......
Osborn & Blood	......	......	......	......	25,000
P. F. McDonough	......	......	......	......	5,000
Dewson, Williams & Co.	......	......	......	......	80,000
S. May, (heirs)	242	46,000	4,000	5,832	......
W. F. Wild	260	19,000	6,000	3,013	......
P. Coffin (heirs)	117	12,000	2,000	1,566	......
B. G. Boardman	127	25,000	4,000	3,628	......
D. A. Ginn & Co.	......	......	......	......	5,000
Nichols & Miller	......	......	......	......	500
J. M. Cook	131	40,000	35,000	5,785	......
T. R. Marvin & Son	......	......	......	......	7,000
Lee & Shepard	......	......	......	......	30,000
White, Osborn & Co	......	......	......	......	7,000
J. Maxwell	147	40,000	40,000	5,800	7,000
H. H. Hunnewell, (trustee)	......	......	......	......	200,000
J. McQunes & Co	153	7,500	2,500	777	......
Sampson & Davenport	......	......	......	......	3,000
H. P. Marston	......	......	......	......	1,500
F. E. Fitts	155	7,500	2,500	765	......
A. H. Read	......	......	......	......	......
" " & Co.o	......	......	......	......	5,000
W. B. Spooner & Co	165	......	......	......	102,400

DETAILS OF LOSSES.

W. B. Spooner		110,000	11,750	......
C. M. Barrett	......	......	......	8,000
A. L. White & Co.	177	20,000	......	112,000
B. G. Boardman	......	......	2,600	......
Nichols & Dalton	......	16,000	......	7,000
Booth & Co.	......	......	......	500
B. G. Boardman	183	34,000	4,800	......
C. M. Holmes	......	......	......	1,000
B. G. Boardman & Co.	......	34,000	......	28,500
M. Dolan & Co	......	......	......	2,000
C. Marsh & Co.	......	......	......	15,000
Henry Poor & Son	189–199	80,000	9,500	......
N. W. Rice & Co.	......	65,000	......	151,100
J. B. Moors	205–211	33,000	3,350	......
G. B. Pearson & Co.	......	32,000	......	3,000
A. Knight	......	......	......	6,000
H. Kitfield & Son	......	......	......	15,000
G. Q. Thorndike	Cor.	15,000	2,000	......
J. P. Preston	Cor.	12,000	1,586	......
"	Cor.	12,000	1,586	......
	237	30,000	3,191	......
J. Hyndman	......	......	......	15,000
W. W. & C. H. Tuttle	233	10,000	1,290	......
Benj. Willis (heirs)	......	8,000	......	6,000
Webster Bros. & Co.	......	......	......	......
L. L. Fuller	227	11,000	1,387	......
C. C. Stevens & Co.	......	9,000	......	2,000
Priest & Alber.	......	......	......	28,700
E. C. Mulliken	223	11,000	1,400	......
W. E. Field & Lawrence	......	9,000	......	25,000
E. W. Cony & Co.	......	......	......	15,000

CONGRESS STREET—Continued.

Names.	Nos.	Value of Land.	Value of Buildings.	Square Feet of Land.	Personal.
S. R. Spaulding	253	$20,000	$10,000	3,033	
G. Plaisted & Son					$27,400
Hinman Meredith (heirs)	26	60,000	5,000	2,200	
W. S. Perry		85,000	60,000	2,584	
H. L. Hallett	36–40	54,000	22,000	1,800	
Mesil & Co					3,000
W. B Carlton					2,000
Storrow & Van Brunt					1,000
F. M. Johnson	46	55,000	20,000	2,000	
C. C. Roberts					2,000
E. F. Page & Co					6,000
G. G. Morris & Co					8,000
F. M. Johnson	44	42,000	13,000	1,530	
Howes & Monks (trustees)	8 Sq.	45,000	20,000	3,053	
D. Dudley & Co					5,000
W. Breese					1,000
C. Lyman	19	30,000	7,000	1,000	
J. P. Kelton					500
C. Lyman	21	30 000	7,000	1,120	
J. M. Robbins	23	32,000	10,000	1,080	
Babb & Stephens					1,000
Cole & Clark					300
S. E. Kendall & Co					5,000
Howes & Monks (trustees)	31	30,000	50,000	845	
" "	33	65,000	15,000	2,600	

DETAILS OF LOSSES.

W. B. Richards	43	24,000	6,000		
Schyer Bros					11,500
S. V. Collins					1,000
Edward Steimle				864	500
J. Quincy (trustees)		18,000	2,000		
Ed. A. White (trustee)		147,000	63,000	4,900	
J. E. Burrick					6,900
Sampson, Davenport & Co					12,000
C. H. Crosby & Co					35,000
W. M. Miller & Co					1,000
E. & F. Dillingham, 50 Water					4,000
James Leeds	70	20,000	5,000	800	
James Parker	66	50,000	40,000	1,500	
H. N. H. Lugrin					400
A. B. Munroe, Jr					2,000
S. B. Wilder & Co					5,000
McKay Sewing Machine Association					117,700
McKay Heeling Association					14,500
Swan & Co					1,800
F. H. Stimpson		48,000	12,000	1,400	4,000
T. W. Ripley & Co	59	60,000	30,000	3,300	
P. B. Brigham					35,000
Dillingham & Co					10,000
J. P. Marshall & Bro					7,000
Lougee & Raymond					14,500
Thomas & Talbot					
Thomas Wigglesworth	65	35,000	18,000	2,000	
J. A. Butler					1,000
Geo. Wheelwright & Son					3,000
J. C. Regan & Co					3,000

CONGRESS STREET—Continued.

Names.	Nos.	Value of Land.	Value of Buildings.	Square Feet of Land.	Personal.
Marple & Shaw	......	......	......	......	$15,000
Spaulding & Co	......	......	......	......	25,000
Exeter Mach. Works	......	......	......	......	1,000
A. D. Brown	......	......	......	......	1,000
Ed. Wigglesworth	69–73	$60,000	$22,000	2,000	......

DEVONSHIRE STREET.

Names.	Nos.	Value of Land.	Value of Buildings.	Square Feet of Land.	Personal.
T. B. Lawrence (heirs)	80–82	$122,000	$60,000	3,700	......
B. F. Bennett & Tilden	......	......	......	......	$6,000
Hagar & Co	......	......	......	......	8,000
G. C. Richardson	98–95	38,000	7,000	1,750	30,000
Mellen & Tillson	......	......	......	......	40,000
Floyd Bros. & Co	......	......	......	......	3,000
Briggs & Co	......	......	......	......	11,400
P. C. Jones & Co	......	......	......	......	75,000
Morse, Johnson & Co	81	30,000	7,000	1,250	......
E. Dwight et als. (trustees)	83	36,000	16,000	1,630	......
Val. Simmons	......	......	......	......	30,000
Burr, Brown & Co	......	......	......	......	75,000
Thos. Sprague & Co	87	36,000	16,000	1,650	......
E. A. White et als. (trustees)	......	......	......	......	70,000
Wheelock, Jones & Co	......	......	......	......	......

DETAILS OF LOSSES.

Name	Pages				
J. L. Tyler					8,000
Geo. S. Curtis	91	36,000	16,000	1,600	
J. B. Palmer & Co					60,000
A. Storrs & Co					45,000
J. H. Curtis	97	36,000	16,000	1,630	17,900
Hunt, Twitchell & Co					
A. Hardy et als. (trustees)	99	36,000	16,000	1,600	17,000
M. C. Hood & Co					30,000
M. Lowry & Co					
Hugh Montgomery	105	34,000	16,000	1,415	25,000
J. H. A. Tappan & Co					
A. Hardy et als. (trustees)	107	40,000	17,000	1,786	60,000
Leland, Rice & Co					
H. H. Hunnewell	136	70,000	45,000	3,150	38,000
Champney Bros. & Co					150,000
Chamberlain & Currier					
Wright & Whiteman	140–146	100,000	65,000	6,602	60,000
Harris, Richardson & Co					130,000
Knowles & Leland					
H. H. Hunnewell	148–152	190,000	125,000	13,203	500,000
Sargent Bros. & Co					284,200
Freeland, Harding & Richardson					
L. Miles Standish	158	36,000	24,000	1,890	75,000
Allen, Lane & Co					1,000
Ezra C. Dyer					
L. Miles Standish	160	36,000	24,000	2,262	80,000
Mason, Tucker & Co					
Nathan Drake	164–166	36,000	24,000	2,158	100,000
D. C. Griswold & Co					
Isaac Rich (heirs)	170–176	50,000	30,000	3,250	

DEVONSHIRE STREET—Continued.

Names.	Nos.	Value of Land.	Value of Buildings.	Square Feet of Land.	Personal.
Odway, Blodgett & Co........	....	....	....	....	$175,000
Sampson, Hale & Co..........	....	....	....	....	25,000
Isaac Rich (heirs)............	178	$50,000	$30,000	3,250	....
Mackentire, Lawrie & Co.....	....	....	....	....	63,300
Isaac Rich (heirs)............	180-184	75,000	45,000	4,346	....
Danforth, Clark & Co.........	....	....	....	....	50,000
Converse, Richardson & Co...	....	....	....	....	100,000
J. C. Burrage & Co...........	....	....	....	....	189,000

FEDERAL STREET.

Names.	Nos.	Value of Land.	Value of Buildings.	Square Feet of Land.	Personal.
Page Belting Co.............	....	....	....	....	$10,000
G. D. Putnam...............	....	....	....	....	2,000
Char'tte A. Johnson.........	9	$40,000	$15,000	2,836	....
"	11	27,000	13,000	2,131	....
Lindsley & Gibbs............	....	....	....	....	40,000
Wells & Wilbur..............	....	....	....	....	5,000
Plum & Atwood Manf. Co....	....	....	....	....	25,000
C. A. Johnson...............	17	27,000	13,000	2,131	....
Holmes, Booth & Hayden.....	....	....	....	....	25,000
J. B. Parker & Co...........	....	....	....	....	10,000
J. H. Beal..................	21	110,000	40,000	7,040	....
Sherburn & Co..............	....	....	....	....	12,000
Hunt, Cox & Kilburn.........	....	....	....	....	12,000
G. H. W. Bates & Co........	....	....	....	....	2,000
Rowe & Waugh (agents)......	....	....	....	....	5,000

DETAILS OF LOSSES.

Leeds & Ross				5,000
G. C. Richardson	27	115,000	7,373	
" " & Co.				50,000
Mann, Bowers & Sawyer				30,000
G. C. Richardson	37	53,000	4,492	
H. Cannerais & Co.				35,000
J. Lawrence et als	43	35,000	2,720	
" " (trustees)	47	65,000	5,040	
J. R. Bigelow & Co.				200,000
Hosmer & Winch Bro.				50,000
C. Merriam (heirs)	51	160,000	9,800	
Webb & Ball				15,900
W. Greenough, Jr.				30,000
Faulkner, Sweet & Co.				3,000
Orderless Rubber Co.				4,500
Melendy, Dexter & Co.				10,000
Melendy, Hixon & Co.				35,000
Gardner Brewer	57	135,000	6,950	23,000
" " & Co.	61			350,000
A. Hamilton & Co.				3,000
Bradford & Young				9,000
D. D. Fisk & Co.	65	80,000	6,094	
J. Ritchie et als				200,000
Jackson, Mandell & Co.	71	62,000		
E. L. Childs			5,550	
Scudder, Rogers & Co.				56,600
H. W. Longfellow, Jr.				12,300
G. T. Bigelow et als	91	88,000	11,848	
C. T. Walker & Co.				15,000
D. Snow	103	40,000	4,255	

FEDERAL STREET—Continued.

Names.	Nos.	Value of Land.	Value of Buildings.	Square Feet of Land.	Personal.
Nichols, Parker & Dupee	......	......	......	......	$100,000
Rogers & Co	......	......	......	......	35,000
Butler, Johnson & Co	113	......	......	......	110,000
Nathan Matthews	"	$52,000	$48,000	5,117	......
Wright, Goodwin & Delano	......	......	......	......	60,000
I. Pratt et als	117	52,000	48,000	5,065	65,000
Chamberlain Bros. & Co	......	......	......	......	55,000
A. W. Clapp & Co	......	......	......	......	......
H. H. Hunnewell	125	63,000	47,000	6,300	6,000
J. Woodman (agent)	......	......	......	......	12,000
Schovill Manf. Co	......	......	......	......	......
J. Revere (administrator)	135	47,000	33,000	4,621	75,000
Wm. Jessop & Sons	......	......	......	......	21,900
Hussey, Wells & Co	......	......	......	......	7,000
F. Q. Strong & Co	......	......	......	......	......
J. Revere (agent)	139	42,000	25,000	4,229	7,000
C. B. Hill (agent)	......	......	......	......	10,000
W. D. Hobbs	......	......	......	......	......
D. L. & J. G. Webster	147	35,000	30,000	3,150	46,900
Welch & Griffith	......	......	......	......	......
S. R. Spaulding	157	60,000	25,000	2,500	......
F. G. & Q. A. Shaw (trustees)	8	75,000	25,000	4,032	2,000
L. Crane	......	......	......	......	100,000
Sanford, Soule & Co	......	......	......	......	......
S. H. Russell (trustee)	10—18	40,000	30,000	2,840	......

DETAILS OF LOSSES.   35

S. H. Russell (trustee)	24	38,000	32,000	3,200	......
Hunt & Russell	......	......	......	......	35,000
Thos. Flint & Co	......	......	......	......	10,000
A. T. Hall	30	40,000	35,000	3,560	......
Banfield, Forristall & Co	......	......	......	......	65,000
E. D. Peters	34	38,000	12,000	3,740	......
Hapgood & Co	......	......	......	......	17,000
Goldthwait & Foster	......	......	......	......	16,000
J. P. Gilman	42	18,000	12,000	1,481	......
B. G. Boardman	46	22,000	8,000	1,859	......
Holway & Co	......	......	......	......	500
Jacob & Averbeck	......	......	......	......	500
Wm. Minot, Jr. (trustee)	54	17,000	10,000	1,280	......
Gammage Bros	......	......	......	......	600
N. Snow	60	19,000	11,000	1,470	......
Wenter & Trask	......	......	......	......	4,100
Ellen M. Abbott et als.	66	40,000	20,000	3,094	......
Bailey & Gilbert	......	......	......	......	6,000
S. P. Baldwin	......	......	......	......	5,000
Benedict & Burnham Manf. Co	......	......	......	......	25,000
Clark & Warren	......	......	......	......	22,000
W. F. Weld	72	40,000	40,000	3,498	......
Stratton, Corey & Co	......	......	......	......	63,100
W. S. Barnes	......	......	......	......	6,000
R. Baker, Jr.	76	40,000	40,000	3,880	......
Hoyt, Wheeler & Bradley	......	......	......	......	25,000
J. H. Osgood	......	......	......	......	50,000
W. Sheafe	80	63,000	62,000	5,623	......
B. Callender & Co	......	......	......	......	71,300
Rothwell, Luther, Potter & Co	......	......	......	......	75,000

FEDERAL STREET—*Continued.*

Names.	Nos.	Value of Land.	Value of Buildings.	Square Feet of Land.	Personal.
Mary Powers (heirs)	86	$44,000	$9,000	4,137	......
J. S. Meyer	......	......	......	......	$500
W. Mitchell	......	......	......	......	500
P. Cushing (heirs)	90	18,000	3,000	1,738	......
Cooper & Co.	......	......	......	......	500
H. & F. A. Whitwell (executor)	98	42,000	35,000	5,280	177,800
Hallowell & Coburn	......	......	......	......	55,000
Frye, Phipps & Co.	......	......	......	......	12,000
J. Collamore	104	40,000	35,000	5,080	28,400
Fairbanks & Allen	......	......	......	......	......
Earl Smith & Co.	......	......	......	......	......
D. Snow	118	43,000	37,000	4,295	47,800
Sabine & Page	......	......	......	......	25,000
Wales, Minot & Co.	......	......	......	......	300,000
Howland, Luce & Co.	......	......	......	......	......
Nathan Matthews	128	90,000	95,000	9,234	200,000
Fenno, Abbott & Co.	......	......	......	......	13,000
Torsliff, Hinckly & Hammond	......	......	......	......	7,900
B. H. Thayer & Co.	......	......	......	......	......
T. Goddard	146	75,000	5,000	9,392	......
M. H. Bancroft	152	14,000	3,000	1,265	500
P. Mullen	......	......	......	......	......
T. Harrington	154	14,000	3,000	1,261	......
Catherine Ford	156	13,000	3,000	1,152	......
C. A. Welch (trustee)	158	14,000	3,000	1,211	......

DETAILS OF LOSSES.

G. W. & F. Smith	164	17,000	16,000	1,408	5,800
Fletcher Manf. Co					400
Thayer, Foote & Co	178–182	28,000	24,000	2,254	25,000
Low, Hersey & Co					15,000
Fernald & Daniels					
Boston Leather Board Co	201	30,000	28,000	3,115	
A. T. Brown					8,800
Burgess, Faxon & Co					500
F. A. Sproul	207	38,000	2,000	7,180	
S. Piper (heirs)					200
A. W. Titus					

FEDERAL COURT.

Jordan, Marsh & Co		$12,000	$1,000	2,550
"		18,000	2,000	3,960

FRANKLIN STREET.

John A. Lowell (trustee)	12–16	$93,000	$65,000	3,700	$75,000
W. H. Horton & Co					30,000
West, Call, Whittemore & Co					
John A. Lowell & Co	18–22	115,000	85,000	6,800	13,100
James L. Little & Co					70,600
James Lovett & Co					
President & Fellows Harvard College	24–28	136,000	100,000	6,800	
White, Brown & Co					450,000

FRANKLIN STREET—Continued.

Names.	Nos.	Value of Land.	Value of Buildings.	Square Feet of Land.	Personal.
Dexter, Abbott & Co.	......	......	......	......	$203,000
Geo. P. Upham.	30–34	$100,000	$60,000	5,050	......
Evans, Webster & Co.	......	......	......	......	85,000
E. O. Tufts & Co.	......	......	......	......	5,000
Mackintosh, Green & Co.	......	......	......	......	40,000
Mary & Ann Wigglesworth.	36–38	72,000	38,000	4,000	......
Almy & Co.	......	......	......	......	80,000
E. Allen & Co.	......	......	......	......	139,900
Mary & Ann Wigglesworth.	40–42	68,000	37,000	3,800	......
Moore, Smith & Co.	......	......	......	......	65,700
Horswell, Kinsley & French.	......	......	......	......	100,000
Wm. Sohier et als (trustees).	44–50	130,000	70,000	6,700	......
Faulkner, Page & Co.	......	......	......	......	800,000
Frost Bros. & Co.	......	......	......	......	80,000
A. Hardy et als (trustees).	54–58	130,000	70,000	7,100	......
Stanfield, Wentworth & Co.	......	......	......	......	150,000
Morse, Sheppard & Co.	......	......	......	......	180,400
A. Hardy et als (trustees).	60–66	156,000	84,000	9,200	......
Isaac Fenno & Co.	......	......	......	......	462,600
Hogan, Clark & Sleeper.	......	......	......	......	60,000
Blake & Stearns.	......	......	......	......	38,800
E. W. Pike.	68–72	62,000	25,000	3,452	......
Rufus S. Frost & Co.	......	......	......	......	40,000
S. H. Pearce & Co.	......	......	......	......	25,000
Dresser, Parsons, Bradt & Co.	......	......	......	......	75,000

DETAILS OF LOSSES.

Name	No.				
A. Hardy et als. (trustees)	74-76	125,000	100,000	4,994	......
Burr, Taft & Co.	......	......	......	......	106,600
Merrill & Lovejoy	......	......	......	......	14,800
John Jeffries, Jr.	7-9	55,000	26,000	2,370	......
Edward Kakas	......	......	......	......	12,000
Kendall, Barrows & Co.	13-15	32,000	18,000	1,459	40,000
Edward D. Peters	......	......	......	......	13,100
Matthew Binney's Sons	......	......	......	......	35,000
Mandell, Burrill & Co.	......	68,000	65,000	3,400	......
Patrick Donahoe	21	86,000	70,000	3,430	125,000
"	25-27	......	......	......	......
F. Skinner & Co.	43	90,000	70,000	6,032	80,000
President & Fellows Harvard Coll.	45-47	......	......	......	302,700
Smith, Stebbens & Co.	......	110,000	75,000	6,032	......
Denny, Rice & Co.	49	......	......	......	300,000
E. A. White et als. (trustees)	51-55	55,000	45,000	3,780	300,000
J. C. Howe & Co.	......	......	......	......	25,000
Leland, Allen & Bates	......	52,000	40,000	3,130	20,000
J. B. Bradlee (trustee)	51-59	115,000	60,000	5,960	......
Jackson, Rice & Vinton	......	......	......	......	198,000
Frothingham & Co.	......	......	......	......	198,600
Saml. Falls (heirs)	63	45,000	30,000	3,050	200,000
Dale Bros. & Co.	31-33	......	......	......	......
E. A. White et als. (trustees)	35	45,000	30,000	3,000	50,000
Burrage Bros. & Co.	35	......	......	......	100,000
Bliss, Whiting, McK. & Co.	37-39	......	......	......	......
Henry Grew	......	......	......	......	39,800
Safford, Nute & Wilson	......	......	......	......	125,000
Gaving & Grew	......	......	......	......	......
Chas. Woodbury	41-43	......	......	......	......
Pierce, Hardy & Co.	43	......	......	......	......
F. Skinner & Co.	......	......	......	......	......

FRANKLIN STREET—*Continued.*

Names.	Nos.	Value of Land.	Value of Buildings.	Square Feet of Land.	Personal.
Wm. Sohier & Co............	65-69	$53,000	$42,000	3,226	....
Metcalf, Pierce & Co........	....	....	....	....	$30,000
Talbot, Wilmarth & Co......	....	....	....	....	90,000
J. S. E. Wright & Co........	....	....	....	....	59,100
Ed. Wigglesworth............	71-73	200,000	90,000	8,000	....
Taylor, Thomas & Co........	....	....	....	....	110,000
Isaac Rich (heirs)............	77-91	234,000	126,000	8,900	168,800
Barnes, Ward & Co..........	....	....	....	....	450,000
Whitton, Burdett & Young..	....	....	....	....	173,500
Keating, Lane & Co..........	....	....	....	....	2,000
J. F. Steele & Co............	....	....	....	....	....

GRIDLEY STREET.

Henry Willis................	15	$4,000	$2,000	876	....
"	17	4,000	2,000	828	....
"	19	4,000	2,000	864	....
"	21	5,000	3,000	888	....

HAWES STREET.

Ogden Codman............	....	$5,000	$500	500	....

HAWLEY STREET.

B. F. Wells................	3	....	....	....	$1,000
C. F. Shimmin et als......	9	$14,000	$8,000	1,200	....
J. Parker..................	15	14,000	8,000	1,200	....
President & Fellows Harvard Coll.....	....	44,000	22,000	4,200	....

DETAILS OF LOSSES.

Whiting & Co	......	......	......	12,000
Hollis & Gunn	......	......	......	4,000
C. B. Botsford & Co	27	30,000	2,860	6,700
M. & A. Wigglesworth	36	......	......	......
E. A. Kelley	......	......	......	500
Gunn & Adams	......	5,000	......	3,000
Kemlo & Owen	......	......	......	2,000
J. H. Osgood & Co	......	......	......	1,000
F. B. Smith & H. Porter	28	35,000	3,473	800
C. V. Bosworth	......	20,000	......	800
S. A. Beckman & Co	......	......	......	2,500
W. C. Demain & Son	......	5,000	......	......
J. B. Dearborn et als	20	25,000	2,511	1,500
J. Grundy	......	......	......	500
G. L. Lincoln	......	5,000	......	300
Moses Wood	......	......	......	3,000
A. E. Steele	......	......	......	......
T. Bartlett (heirs)	12	12,000	1,200	......

HIGH STREET.

Henry Bond	47	$29,000	$23,000	......
Healy, Farnum & Co	......	......	......	$73,500
Chester Guild & Son	51	24,000	22,000	7,200
Bradford, Kinsley & Co	......	......	2,423	15,000
D. L. & J. G. Webster	57	40,000	35,000	......
E. K. Butler & Brother	......	......	4,051	38,000
J. L. Webster	......	......	......	8,000

HIGH STREET—Continued.

Names.	Nos.	Value of Land.	Value of Buildings.	Square Feet of Land.	Personal.
J. S. Stone	61	$25,000	$22,000	2,552	
W. C. Child					$12,000
Lane, Pierce & Co					15,000
J. O. Cummings & Co					2,000
Stimpson & Phalan					10,000
S. & W. Atherton	65	26,000	23,000	2,619	
H. Billings & Son					85,000
J. & W. Tucker	69	27,000	23,000	2,787	
P. D. Moore & Co					30,000
Brown & Caller					15,000
G. F. Breed					45,000
L. S. Jones	73	29,500	25,500	2,954	
Adams, Low & Newton					50,000
Marsh Brothers					20,000
Wilson & Merrill					60,000
Linnell, Houston & Co					2,500
E. B. Phillips	77	43,000	35,000	4,357	
J. B. Alley & Co					37,000
Merriam & Norton					10,000
Hood & Emerson					20,000
S. E. Wescott	83	34,000	26,000	3,408	
B. F. Thompson & Co					50,000
S. Wescott & Son					275,000
Henry Bond	87	18,000	12,000	1,635	
" " & Co					175,000

DETAILS OF LOSSES.

Name	No.				
Hannah Terrill	......	18,000	......	......	......
Boston Carpet Slipper Co	......	......	......	......	2,500
M. T. Durrill	93	19,000	1,685	12,000	......
S. Snow & Co	93	......	1,796	14,000	......
J. Childs, Jr	95	......	......	......	25,000
J. G. Bartholmesey & Co	......	......	......	......	8,000
S. N. Dickerman & Co	......	......	......	......	7,000
S. R. Spaulding	99	53,000	......	......	8,000
Davis Brothers & Co	101–103	......	4,235	32,000	......
E. Spaulding & Bumstead	2–6	55,000	......	......	40,000
Stephen Dow	......	......	......	......	150,000
Loring & Reynolds	......	55,000	4,842	40,000	......
Stephen Dow	8–12	32,000	2,841	23,000	70,000
E. & A. Mudge & Co	......	......	......	......	21,600
C. F. Ellis & Co	......	......	......	......	12,000
J. H. Lee & Co	......	......	......	......	......
Stephen Dow & Co	......	......	......	......	7,600
F. S. Fay	14–20	55,000	5,092	40,000	......
Martin & Skinner	......	......	......	......	25,000
A. & G. W. Belcher	......	......	......	......	1,000
C. F. Parker & Co	......	......	......	......	28,100
Blake, Higbee & Co	......	......	......	......	2,500
M. B. Sewall (heirs)	24–28	55,000	5,092	40,000	......
Howard & Page	......	......	......	......	2,000
J. Lewis & Co	......	......	......	......	8,000
Perry, Cutter & Co	......	......	......	......	20,000
Geo. P. Sewall & Co	......	......	......	......	4,000
E. H. Sampson	36	40,000	1,905	35,000	......
F. Evans	42	12,000	987	6,000	......
"	46	12,000	872	6,000	......

HIGH STREET—Continued.

Names.	Nos.	Value of Land.	Value of Buildings.	Square Feet of Land.	Personal.
Levi A. Turner					$10,000
W. & E. Sawyer					37,200
Sheriff & Stone					7,000
Jarvis Howe					1,000
J. B. Glover	50	$12,000	$6,000	1,074	
"	52-54	12,000	6,000	1,373	
Howe & Living					6,000
G. G. Good					4,000
B. & A. Foley					30,000
A. Sternfield & Bro					25,600
J. B. Glover	58	12,000	6,000	1,083	
L. Goodnew					7,000
A. P. Learoyd					3,000
Jackson & Loring					5,000
M. H. Gleason	1-5	11,000	20,000	625	
Stellings, Hammond & Co					4,000
J. C. Haynes	7-13	46,000	34,000	3,118	
J. A. & W. S. Lord					12,000
E. Cummings & Co					3,000
Wm. Tidd & Co					30,000
O. H. Underhill & Co					12,000
F. S. Merritt					40,000
T. W. & S. P. Hersey					5,000
J. W. Wheelwright	15	16,000	12,000	1,140	
Phinney & Phillips					12,000

DETAILS OF LOSSES.

N. E. Leman, Jr.............	......	....	....	....	2,000
Leonard Ware................	19	44,000	33,000	3,100	....
"	21	29,000	19,000	1,200	....
Cragin, Page & Co...........	......	....	....	....	77,200
Nichols, McKennedy & Stroud.	......	....	....	....	40,000
C. M. Lee....................	......	....	....	....	7,000
E. R. Swasey & Co...........	25	....	....	....	15,000
Low, Hersey & Co............	27–29	35,000	25,000	2,868	43,900
J. S. Stone..................	31	30,000	23,000	2,614	....
Pelton, Snell & Co...........	......	....	....	....	40,000
Abbott, Loring & Co.........	......	....	....	....	8,000
H. Newhall & Co.............	......	....	....	....	25,000
H. Flanders.................	35	29,000	23,000	2,542	....
J. B. Wehn & Co.............	......	....	....	....	5,000
Geo. S. Hall.................	......	....	....	....	2,500
Hill & Brown................	......	....	....	....	12,000
Jenkins Bros. & Co..........	......	....	....	....	5,000
David Snow..................	39	29,000	23,000	2,859	....
Higbee, Foster & Co.........	......	....	....	....	45,000
W. H. Hurd..................	......	....	....	....	2,000
Kennan, French & Co........	......	....	....	....	7,000
Hawkins, Clay & Brett.......	......	....	....	....	5,000
O. F. Belcher...............	......	....	....	....	1,500
Daniel Johnson..............	43	29,000	23,000	2,810	....
" & Co............	......	....	....	....	46,000
S. O. Pollard & Co...........	......	....	....	....	2,500
M. T Durrell................	62	22,000	16,000	1,815	....
J. Souther, Jr. & Co.........	......	....	....	....	2,500
E. B. Hull & Co.............	......	....	....	....	40,000

HIGH STREET—*Continued.*

Names.	Nos.	Value of Land.	Value of Buildings.	Square Feet of Land.	Personal.
M. T. Durrell	66	$23,000	$18,000	1,860	......
Gay, Dana & Co.	......	......	......	......	$18,000
A. P. Nash & Co.	......	......	......	......	21,000
A. Tirrell	68	25,000	20,000	2,045	......
J. Field	72	40,000	25,000	3,976	......
Allen & Field	......	......	......	......	192,000
S. S. Arnold	78	33,000	22,000	3,335	......
J. P. Rogers & Co.	......	......	......	......	11,000
Converse & Stanwood	......	......	......	......	15,000
E. & A. B. Burgess	82	31,500	21,500	3,205	......
Day, Wilcox & Co.	......	......	......	......	160,000
E. & A. B. Burgess	86	30,500	21,500	......	......
Winslow Brothers	......	......	......	......	1,000
Otis & Bragdon	......	......	......	......	1,000
Noble & Brooks	......	......	......	......	60,000
L. Fletcher & Co.	......	......	......	......	8,000
Foster & Molineaux	......	......	......	......	2,800
J. M. & F. Jones	90	30,000	21,000	2,975	......
E. A. Mansfield	......	......	......	......	3,500
Treadwell, Dugan & Osgood	......	......	......	......	50,000
J. Skinner & Co.	......	......	......	......	8,000
Stillman, Alger & Co.	......	......	......	......	7,000
Hubbard & Blake	......	......	......	......	15,000
E. G. Cook	......	......	......	......	20,000

DETAILS OF LOSSES.

McConnell & Gardner					30,000
T. E. Proctor	94	26,000	18,000	2,616	
J. B. Moors		39,000	36,000	3,606	30,000
" " & Co					5,000
Flint & Clatur					65,000
Homer Wyeth					3,000
C. L. Hathaway & Sons					122,700
T. E. Proctor	106	55,000	25,000	3,970	
" "	110	19,000	9,000	1,680	
" "	114	18,000	11,000	1,638	
" "	118	17,000	10,000	1,512	
Richardson, Doyle & Co					12,000
E. W. Whitemore					5,000
N. N. & C. H. James					20,000
H. Conn & Co					6,600
Knowlton & Lane					5,000
W. C. Boyd & Sons					54,600
P. Lennox & Co	43				5,000
Winn, Eaton & Co					1,500
A. Waite					4,000
R. W. Ames & Co.,	45				27,000
W. Butterfield & Co					25,000

KILBY STREET.

Moses Williams	65	$23,000	$7,000	1,500
" "	67	22,000	7,000	1,500

KILBY STREET—Continued.

Names.	Nos.	Value of Land.	Value of Buildings.	Square Feet of Land.	Personal.
Moses Williams	71	$35,000	$10,000	4,400	......
B. W. Conant & Co	......	......	......	......	$10,000
C. Perry	......	......	......	......	2,000
H. C. Thacher & Co	......	......	......	......	50,000
Capitol Oil Co	......	......	......	......	500
Manning & Sears	......	......	......	......	100,000
I. B. Cobb	......	......	......	......	1,000
Chas. Lyman	75	18,000	7,000	1,400	......
Robert Scott & Co	......	......	......	......	30,000
Binney & Co	......	......	......	......	2,500
Noyes & Poole	......	......	......	......	1,200
Geo. Blackburn. (heirs)	81	19,000	6,000	1,507	......
Hiram Whittington & Co	......	......	......	......	18,000
C. F. S. Townsend	83	18,000	5,000	1,405	......
Samuel Atherton	87–89	18,000	8,000	1,600	......
"	93	28,000	17,000	1,420	......
Boston Type Foundry	......	......	......	......	2,500
J. A. Lynch & Co	......	......	......	......	20,000
Tillson & Co	......	......	......	......	10,000
John Belknap (heirs)	64	18,000	6,000	900	......
Parrott & Co	......	......	......	......	2,000
— Wallis	......	......	......	......	2,000
Daniel P. Stone	58–62	18,000	7,000	900	......
A. R. Smith & Co	......	......	......	......	20,000
Morrill, Whitmore & Co	......	......	......	......	3,900

DETAILS OF LOSSES.

Adams & Chute	......	......	......	5,000
D. Webster, King & Co.	......	......	......	18,000
Andrew C. Spring & Co.	52	......	......	50,000
J. M. Codman	48	19,000	7,000	868	......
Stebenson & Pearson	......	......	......	36,000
J. M. Codman	44	20,000	7,000	785	......
J. W. Seaver & Co.	44	......	......	......	30,000
Young & Emmons	42½	......	......	......	115,000
Broda, Keller & Nutting	......	......	......	2,000
Barber Bros. & Gardiner	......	......	......	1,500
J. W. Hodgdon	40	......	......	300
Wannamacher & Co.	......	......	......	1,000
Richard Codman	38	24,000	8,000	1,118	......
H. A. Johnson & R. Codman	27	40,000	10,000	1,920	......
Gray & Co.	......	......	......	5,000
Whitney, Cushing & Co.	......	......	......	15,000
John Borrowscale & Son	......	......	......	1,000
J. J. Dixwell & E. S. Rand	31	55,000	25,000	2,100	......
R. Codman et als. (trustees)	37	65,000	35,000	2,750	......
Dodge, Gilbert & Co.	......	......	......	100,000
Williams & Hall	......	......	......	50,000
I. G. Whitney & Co.	......	......	......	160,000
J. Phillips (heirs)	43	37,000	15,000	2,000	......
Thayer, Babson & Co.	......	......	......	12,000
J. Phillips (heirs)	55	42,000	20,000	2,000	......
Bagley, Rollins & Co.	......	......	......	35,000
Moses Williams	61	35,000	12,000	1,500	......
I. Porter & Co.	......	......	......	5,000
A. N. Clark & Co.	......	......	......	37,000
C. Varney	......	......	......	1,000

LEATHER SQUARE.

Names.	Nos.	Value of Land.	Value of Buildings.	Square Feet of Land.	Personal.
T. C. Amory (agent)	......	$5,000	$2,000	1,250	......
"	......	5,000	2,000	1,250	......

LINCOLN STREET.

Names.	Nos.	Value of Land.	Value of Buildings.	Square Feet of Land.	Personal.
Lucy A. Harris	2	$11,000	$11,000	1,394	......
C. L. Fowle	......	......	......	......	$500
J. H. J. Hinckle	4	13,000	14,000	1,800	......
Palmer Williams & Co.	......	......	......	......	8,000
James Barrett	6	13,000	20,000	1,875	......

LINDALL STREET.

Names.	Nos.	Value of Land.	Value of Buildings.	Square Feet of Land.	Personal.
J. F. Mills	10	$30,000	$10,000	1,650	......
Geo. O. Smith	......	......	......	......	$2,000
M. C. Ferris	8, 6	17,000	8,000	800	......
C. A. Sutton	......	......	......	......	1,000
Ogden Codman	7	55,000	20,000	3,749	......
M. A. Dow	......	......	......	......	30,000
A. Steam Guage Co.	......	......	......	......	13,000
Richard Codman	9	52,000	30,000	5,858	......
C. L. Allen	......	......	......	......	1,600
H. S. Hastings	......	......	......	......	1,500

DETAILS OF LOSSES.

MATTHEWS STREET.

S. S. Arnold	....	$21,500	....	3,496	$40,000
D. Snow	....	15,000	....	2,516	....

MERCHANTS' EXCHANGE.

Total Value	....	$450,000	$100,000	1,700	....

MILK STREET.

N. L. Williams	5–7	$53,000	$10,000	1,280	$1,500
W. F. Sherman & Co	....	....	....	....	1,000
McCready & Kennedy	....	....	....	....	700
O. H. Osborne	....	....	....	....	1,000
G. Bartholomez & Co	....	28,000	7,000	730	....
J. Bumstead (heirs)	11	....	....	....	200
W. H. Brickett	....	....	....	....	1,500
C. E. Campbell	....	....	....	....	....
D. L. Shepen & Co	15–17	60,000	32,000	2,900	50,000
Ordway Bros. & Co	....	....	....	....	8,000
C. M. Parker	....	....	....	....	46,200
Brewer & Tileston	19–28	108,000	20,000	6,000	....
Mary T. Goddard	....	....	....	....	5,000
V. J. Messenger & Co	....	....	....	....	3,000
F. K. Daggett & Co	....	....	....	....	50,000
Wm. Hecker & Co	....	....	....	....	3,000
Wm. C. Donald & Co	....	....	....	....	....
Jacob Sleeper	27–35	155,000	85,000	11,360	....

MILK STREET—*Continued.*

Names.	Nos.	Value of Land.	Value of Buildings.	Square Feet of Land.	Personal.
Carter Bros. & Co.	......	......	......	......	$45,000
Sleeper, Fisk & Co.	......	......	......	......	35,000
Ed. L. Day	......	......	......	......	2,500
Henry A. Hall	......	......	......	......	35,000
Ed. Dwight et als. (trustees)	37–43	$95,000	$65,000	4,750	68,600
H. & J. Pfaff	......	......	......	......	1,000
C. A. Hovey & Co.	......	......	......	......	8,000
M. W. Carr & Co.	......	......	......	......	214,100
Rice, Kendall & Co.	......	......	......	......	40,000
Lee & Shepard	......	......	......	......	......
Geo. P. Upham	45–47	96,000	44,000	3,200	75,000
Despeaux, Blake & Co.	......	......	......	......	50,800
D. P. Ives & Co.	......	......	......	......	......
T. Biglow Lawrence (heirs)	59	70,000	15,000	3,025	45,000
Cushing & Bliss	55	......	......	......	40,000
French & Coffin	59	......	......	......	......
G. F. & D. W. Williams	63	21,000	6,000	825	6,000
Richard L. Gay & Co.	......	......	......	......	40,000
A. S. March & Co.	......	......	......	......	......
R. T. Paine et als.	67	30,000	5,000	1,510	20,000
C. H. Dunham & Co.	......	......	......	......	20,000
Walker, Short & Co.	......	......	......	......	......
J. S. Cunningham (heirs)	71	50,000	20,000	2,210	60,000
Dinnison & Co.	......	......	......	......	......
H. J. Hallgreen (agent)	......	......	......	......	2,000

DETAILS OF LOSSES

F. G. & Q. A. Shaw (trustees)	77	75,000		
Francis Mallon	77			38,000
Wright & Potter	79			26,000
O. J. Rand				4,000
Levi L. Town	81	55,000	3,241	
S. W. Wilder				2,000
Joy & Gibson				16,000
Conant & Newhall				2,500
Geo. Coleman & Co.				2,000
Cutter, Tower & Co.				100,000
Joseph G. Russell	85	50,000	2,563	
Gray, Palmer & Pendergast				1,000
J. A. & N. Harwood				5,000
Branden Scale Co.				10,000
D. H. Sparhawk & Co.				20,000
Jos. Whitney (heirs)	93	80,000	6,748	
H. M. Clark & Co.				57,700
S. D. Warren & Co.				100,000
Thos. G. Caldwell & Co.	99	32,000		20,100
David W. Williams	99		2,226	
Geo. P. Osborn & Co.	103			15,000
Henry J. Holbrook	105			15,000
Fred. W. Holland	107	32,000	2,226	
Trustees of Tufts Coll.	109	38,000	3,147	
Gilman Bros.				33,000
J. H. Pierce, Robertson & Clark	111			51,000
J. Lawrence & Co. (trustees)	113	32,000	3,395	
A. Hardy et als. (trustees)	117	32,000	3,518	
Eaton, Harrington & Dana				125,000
W. A. Wood & Co.	119			5,000

54 THE BOSTON FIRE.

MILK STREET—Continued.

Names.	Nos.	Value of Land.	Value of Buildings.	Square Feet of Land.	Personal.
Edward Clark (heirs)	121	$40,000	$10,000	3,025	......
Foster, Colburn & Co.	......	......	......	......	$100,000
Thos. Wigglesworth	125	33,000	12,000	2,300	......
"	131	36,000	14,000	2,270	......
Gould, Hitchcock & Co.	......	......	......	......	50,000
H. A. Gould	......	......	......	......	1,000
Thos. Goddard (trustee)	58	42,000	32,000	1,260	......
Ross, Pierce & Co.	......	......	......	......	48,100
Edward Wigglesworth	62	35,000	10,000	1,450	......
T. Curtis & Co.	......	......	......	......	20,000
Edward Wigglesworth	64–66	35,000	10,000	2,000	......
G. W. B. Taylor	......	......	......	......	3,700
Parker & Holden	......	......	......	......	1,000
Holden Bros.	......	......	......	......	1,000
James Leeds	72–74	36,000	12,000	1,200	......
Wm. Mills & Co.	......	......	......	......	12,000
James Leeds	76–78	20,000	5,000	1,050	......
Hyde, Hutchinson & Co.	76–78	......	......	......	60,000
James Lawrence	80–82	90,000	60,000	5,000	......
J. P. Flagg & Co.	......	......	......	......	600
Hill, Clark & Co.	......	......	......	......	11,200
Ellen Stearns	84–86	50,000	20,000	2,350	......
Webster & Co.	......	......	......	......	156,000
A. P. Tapley & Co.	......	......	......	......	40,000
Moses Williams	88	40,000	15,000	1,900	......

DETAILS OF LOSSES.

Hayden, Guardenier & Co.	......	......	......	30,000
Moses Williams	90–92	36,000	1,875	140,000
Francis Dane & Co.	......	......	......	20,000
Varney, Henderson & Co.	......	......	......	15,000
I. G. Swett & Co.	......	......	......	20,000
Ed. Henshaw & Co.	......	......	......	5,000
Tripp, Eddy & Co.	......	......	12,000	......
Thos. Cordis (heirs)	96–98	40,000	2,700	10,000
Alden & Edmands	......	......	13,000	......
R. C. Waterson	100	40,000	3,476	35,000
Wilder & Co.	......	......	15,000	13,000
Thos. Grundy & Co.	......	......	......	39,600
Homer, Bishop & Co.	112	......	......	100,000
D. R. Whitney & Co.	110	......	......	5,000
W. H. Bowdlear	108	......	......	50,000
E. E. Rice & Co.	......	208,000	92,000	......
Liberty Sqr. Warehouse Co.	......	......	......	1,000
W. Baily, Lang & Co.	......	......	1,300	1,000
J. A. Waldo	5–7	......	......	11,000
D. W. Holmes & Co.	1–3	28,000	12,000	......
Benj. F. White	......	......	1,100	5,000
Stimson & Babcock	......	......	......	7,000
Jenkins & Co.	......	......	......	200,000
Lyons & Vose	......	......	......	......

MILTON PLACE.

J. Revere (administrator)	4	$4,500	$3,000	......
" "	5	4,500	3,000	......
I. Rich (heirs)	1	60,000	30,000	......
S. W. Fowle & Sons	......	......	13,310	$10,000

MORTON PLACE.

NAMES.	Nos.	Value of Land.	Value of Buildings.	Square Feet of Land.	Personal.
M. & A. Wigglesworth	3	$10,000	$6,000	6,000	......
S. Hatch & Co.	......	......	......	......	$5,000
D. K. Chase	......	......	......	......	3,000
W. Crocker	13	10,000	6,000	1,650	......
N. F. Howard	......	......	......	......	200
T. C. Amory (agent)	15	10,000	6,000	1,650	......
T. Carroll & Co.	......	......	......	......	3,500
W. G. Blood	......	......	......	......	2,000
F. C. Anthus & Co.	......	......	......	......	500
T. C. Amory (agent)	19	10,000	6,000	1,650	......
A. Hardy et als. (trustees)	23–25	13,000	12,000	1,830	......
J. J. Bukmaier & Burns	......	......	......	......	5,000
W. Sohier et als.	27	11,000	9,000	1,900	......
G. W. Manning	......	......	......	......	200

OLIVER STREET.

NAMES.	Nos.	Value of Land.	Value of Buildings.	Square Feet of Land.	Personal.
Thos. Wigglesworth	7–9	$15,000	$5,000	1,254	......
Abbott & Howard	......	......	......	......	$150,000
Wm. G. Lincoln	11	33,000	20,000	3,258	......
Trustees Boston University	13–17	18,000	15,000	1,633	......
"	"	14,000	13,000	1,422	......
W. G. Lincoln	29	46,000	34,000	4,791	......

OTIS STREET.

Elias B. Paine (heirs)	1–3	$25,000	$10,000	......
" "	4–6	35,000	10,000	$15,000
E. W. Holbrook & Co.	1–2	......	......	15,000
H. F. Champney	.3	......	......	10,000
E. Skinner & Co.	4	......	......	4,500
A. B. Crocker	5	......	......	......
C. Clemment & Co.	6	......	......	12,000
Stephen B Simmons	7–8	45,000	35,000	2,470
Simmons Bros. & Co.	......	......	......	75,000
Foster Waterman (heirs)	9–10	80,000	55,000	4,600
March Bros., Pierce & Co.	......	......	......	130,000
Miner, Beal & Hackett	11	......	......	300,000
Hawley & Folsom	13	80,000	55,000	4,340
Hawley, Folsom & Martin	......	......	......	172,800
Henry B. Williams (attorney)	14	74,000	51,000	4,134
Thos. Kelly & Co.	15	......	......	100,000
D. M. Hodgdon & Co.	......	......	......	88,200
Boston Star Collar Co.	......	......	......	4,000
Sibley, Cummer & Co.	16	......	......	60,000
Farr, Hatch & Co.	25	......	......	20,000
Green Bros. & Co.	24	......	......	50,000

PEARL STREET.

J. P. Cushing (heirs)	1	$170,000	$30,000	8,500
T. S. Nowell	......	......	......	$30,000
Rogers, Corry & Co.	......	......	......	20,000

3*

PEARL STREET—Continued.

NAMES.	Nos.	Value of Land.	Value of Buildings.	Square Feet of Land.	Personal.
J. H. Power & Co.	......	......	......	......	$300
A. & G. A. Kendall	3–5	$30,000	$20,000	2,640	......
J. Ireson & Son	......	......	......	......	18,000
Jenkins, Knight & Wood	......	......	......	......	10,000
J. Lawrence (trustee)	7	30,000	20,000	2,469	......
W. White	11	......	......	......	7,000
I. W. Howe & Co.	......	......	......	......	150,000
T. B. Lawrence (heirs)	13	45,000	25,000	5,036	110,000
G. B. Wentworth	......	......	......	......	1,000
Parker, Bryant & Co.	......	......	......	......	1,000
D. H. Darling & Co.	......	......	......	......	4,000
Cole, Wood & Co.	......	......	......	......	75,000
T. B. Lawrence (heirs)	17	30,000	20,000	2,520	......
D. Harwood & Co.	......	......	......	......	31,700
E. Potter & Co.	......	......	......	......	9,700
W. Ames & Co.	......	......	......	......	5,000
J. Leeds	23	50,000	26,000	2,520	......
Whitcombe & Thayer	......	......	......	......	19,700
J. O'Connell	......	......	......	......	4,000
R. Hayes & Co.	......	......	......	......	5,000
C. & M. Cox	......	......	......	......	100,000
Chase, Merritt & Blanchard	......	......	......	......	85,000
Edson & Searvens	......	......	......	......	11,400
J. K. Mullen & Co.	......	......	......	......	9,500
B. E. Faxon & Co.	......	......	......	......	1,200

DETAILS OF LOSSES.

L. Blanchard				1,000
Skilton & Dole				65,000
W. A. Kelley & Son				4,000
Thayer & Brother				50,000
S. S. Perkins	12	55,000	25,000	4,400
Hecht Bros. & Co				35,000
W. A. Shaw				8,000
J. Tappan (heirs)	4	37,000	20,000	2,268
T. J. Howe & Co				4,000
J. Perry & Co				2,500
A. N. Saunders & Co	27			20,000
Thos. Mims et als	29	27,000	13,000	2,457
Nelson Emmons & Co				35,000
Tenny Aldrich & Co				130,000
S. C. Wheelwright	33	27,000	13,000	2,457
Field, Thayer & Whitcomb				125,000
S. Gilman & Co				70,000
J. J. Henry				30,000
Z. B. Adams (heirs)	37	27,000	15,000	2,457
Coring, Putnam & Co				10,000
C. W. Forbush & Co				5,000
J. Edmands				1,500
C. H. Young & Co				13,300
Caleb Stetson	41	27,000	13,000	2,457
M. & J. Wallace				100,000
B. F. Spillman & Co				20,000
E. Tucker & Son				1,000
S. W. Atherton	45	27,000	13,000	2,457
Cowing & Hatch				25,200
A. A. Pope & Co				30,000

PEARL STREET—Continued.

Names.	Nos.	Value of Land.	Value of Buildings.	Square Feet of Land.	Personal.
Wales Tucker.............	49	$27,000	$13,000	2,457	......
S. B. Stone & Co........	......	......	......	......	$51,200
A. Curtis...................	......	......	......	......	12,000
Thos. Emerson's Sons..	......	......	......	......	5,000
J. Leeds....................	53	25,000	11,000	1,650	......
Sears & Warner..........	......	......	......	......	65,000
Freeman Allen (heirs).	55	35,000	25,000	3,500	......
Holmes, Harlow & Co.	......	......	......	......	4,000
B. Blanchard & Co......	......	......	......	......	4,000
Potter, White & Bayley.	......	......	......	......	200,000
E. & A. H. Batchelder & Co.	67	......	......	......	300,000
C. A. Torry................	69	......	......	......	7,000
Hoyt & Parker............	......	......	......	......	2,500
J. Fairbanks (heirs).....	67	50,000	35,000	4,080	......
Ed. Brooks.................	69	40,000	25,000	3,323	......
J. F. Dane, Grinnell & Co.	......	......	......	......	150,000
Hill & Rowe...............	......	......	......	......	5,000
Ed. Brooks.................	71	38,000	22,000	3,549	......
Robbins & Kellogg.....	......	......	......	......	1,000
Cummings & Redman.	......	......	......	......	1,500
A. M. Bigelow & Co....	......	......	......	......	40,000
Samuel Sparhawk.......	77	......	......	......	500
Ed. Brooks.................	......	27,000	18,000	2,610	......
I. P. Pope..................	......	......	......	......	500
B. F. Campbell...........	......	......	......	......	50,000

DETAILS OF LOSSES.

Bond & Tidd				2,000
Ed. Brooks	81	55,000	45,000	5,714
Chockran & Thayer				20,600
H. H. Mawhinny & Co.				10,000
Wm. Claflin & Co.				60,000
Ed. Brooks	85	35,000	25,000	3,421 42,500
J. Wooldredge & Co.				35,000
Johnson, Rust & Co.				25,000
F. S. Wheeler & Co.	89			
Ed. Brooks				2,000
I. N. Merriam & Son	91	30,000	22,000	2,822
Clapp & Billings				50,000
Ed. Brooks	93	60,000	50,000	6,258
Harrington & Cummings				75,000
J. Cummings, Jr. & Co.				71,500
J. H. Putnam & Wheeler				19,500
W. H. Phipps & Co.				6,000
L. H. Bowker & Co.				6,000
E. L. Thayer				500
Stowe, Bills & Whitney				40,000
A. Aldrich & Son				5,000
W. G. Perry				500
Alex. Strong	97	34,000	28,000	3,064
Rousmaniere & Kimball				36,100
C. H. Dill				2,500
Wm. Burrage (heirs)	99	32,000	28,000	2,828
E. A. Strong & Burt				97,300
H. L. Daggett & Co.	107	60,000	45,000	4,461
I. M. & Frederick Jones				300,000
J. B. Kimball & Co.				110,200

PEARL STREET—Continued.

Names.	Nos.	Value of Land.	Value of Buildings.	Square Feet of Land.	Personal.
J. Richardson et als. (heirs)	109	$29,000	$18,000	1,680	
Brooks & Young	58				$35,000
American Shoe Tip Co					50,000
Pat. Shoe Stay Co					13,500
W. S. Batchelder					10,000
W. H. Bordman	54	23,000	15,000	1,983	
Crane, Leland & Moody					10,000
Rhodes, Paige & Co					80,000
J. M. Smith	50	14,000	12,000	1,112	
D. Parker & Co					150,000
J. Comer (trustee)	48	16,000	7,000	828	
Thing & Norris					35,000
J. Parker	40	78,000	42,000	6,639	
Nash, French & Co					8,000
J. W. Barnard					4,000
Badger & Manny					60,000
Lyman Dike					5,000
E. C. Bailey					2,500
Holbrook, Hobart & Potter					3,000
S. Blake & Co					2,000
Mallard & Butler					10,000
N. Sylvester					1,000
J. Parker	34	50,000	25,000	5,445	
Houghton & Hayward					10,000
A. Fellows					3,000

DETAILS OF LOSSES.

Atherton, Stetson & Co.				200,000
E. Cruft (heirs)	32	85,000	45,000	9,535
D. C. Perrin & Co.				2,000
Mann & Brackett				20,000
Jenny & Co.				1,000
E. W. & G. W. W. Littlefield				500
C. F. Barnes				800
Spraguir & McKey				15,200
Johnson & Tewksbury				30,000
C. H. Ward				35,000
Haven & Wright				45,000
Knowlton & James				8,000
T. White & Co				40,000
Ed. Cruft (heirs)	20	60,000	35,000	6,720
I. A. Nay & Co.				2,500
Ed. Downing				14,000
E. P. Phillips & Co.				40,000
Davis, Rook & Pope				2,000
W. E. Putnam & Co.				30,000
J. McGregor	90	40,000	35,000	4,030
Claflin & Thayer				151,000
J. Hill & Co.				22,500
J. Swan & Co.				3,000
Ed. Forness & Co.				3,000
Chas. Lane	84	38,000	30,000	3,875
C. W. Webster & Co.				4,000
A. C. Mayhew & Co.				1,600
J. Harris & Sons				10,000
Shaw, Taylor & Co.				5,000
R. E. Emerson				25,000

PEARL STREET—Continued.

Names.	Nos.	Value of Land.	Value of Buildings.	Square Feet of Land.	Personal.
C. F. Allen	......	......	......	......	$1,500
N. D. Canterbury	......	......	......	......	2,500
D. Denny (heirs)	78	......	......	......	......
Loring, Searl & Co.	......	$40,000	$30,000	4,030	48,800
T. S. Ruddick	......	......	......	......	3,000
Harvey & Daniels	......	......	......	......	31,000
A. B. Harvey & Co.	......	......	......	......	20,000
D. Denny (heirs)	74	38,000	20,000	3,875	......
Lucius Bulse	......	......	......	......	30,000
D. G. Rawson & Co.	......	......	......	......	5,000
D. Denny (heirs)	70	40,000	30,000	4,030	200,000
Fogg, Houghton & Coolidge	......	......	......	......	......
D. Denny (heirs)	66	65,000	50,000	6,173	125,000
J. & D. W. Hitchcock	......	......	......	......	12,000
J. Durgin & Son	......	......	......	......	13,200
Z. Einstein Bros. & Co.	......	......	......	......	22,000
A. P. Conant & Co.	......	......	......	......	1,500
J. D. Pike & Co.	......	......	......	......	3,000
A. A Gilmore & Co.	......	......	......	......	1,500
Jefts & Davis	......	......	......	......	1,000
J. M. Watson & Co.	58	29,000	16,000	1,983	......
J. C. Dodge (heirs)	......	......	......	......	150,000
Ruinn & Edwards	113–115	20,000	15,000	1,537	......
J. A. Bacon	......	......	......	......	102,900
J. Tucker & Co.	......	......	......	......	......

DETAILS OF LOSSES.

B. Hammatt	117	19,000	15,000	1,600	......
D. C. Buffum	......	......	......	......	101,000
A. B. Keith & Co.	......	......	......	......	......
B. Hammatt	121	18,000	15,000	1,600	40,000
Lester, Johnson & Moody	......	......	......	......	40,000
J. W. Brigham & Co.	......	......	......	......	54,500
Clement, Colburn & Co.	125	18,000	15,000	1,584	100,000
C. B. Lancaster	......	......	......	......	5,000
I. D. Richards	129	18,000	14,000	1,544	......
E. & M. Faxon	......	......	......	......	35,000
J. M. Jones	133	17,000	14,000	1,512	......
Burrage & Reed	......	......	......	......	40,000
Hilton & Grover	......	......	......	......	4,000
J. W. Robinson & Co.	......	......	......	......	3,000
I. Williams (heirs)	137	16,000	14,000	1,509	......
Brown & Goodwin	......	......	......	......	10,000
J. D. Whicher & Co.	......	......	......	......	15,000
S. B. Phillips	......	......	......	......	8,000
Albert Tirrell	143	16,000	14,000	1,740	25,000
F. H. Kidder & Co.	......	......	......	......	......
J. C. Bucknam	145	16,000	14,000	1,740	2,000
Hiram Temple	......	......	......	......	20,000
C. Howe & Co.	......	......	......	......	......
Betsey Terrill	149	20,000	16,000	1,820	......
J. & A. Terrill & Co.	......	......	......	......	66,900
E. B. Phillips	153–169	115,000	80,000	15,773	......
Coon, Crocker & Hobart	......	......	......	......	43,000
Bryant & King	......	......	......	......	25,000
Nichols, Lovejoy & Co.	......	......	......	......	3,900
Hitchcock & Archer	......	......	......	......	5,000

PEARL STREET—Continued.

Names.	Nos.	Value of Land.	Value of Buildings.	Square Feet of Land.	Personal.
J. Brackett & Co.					$1,000
P. Ware, Jr. & Co.					125,000
W. F. Weld & Co.	160	$65,000	$10,000	10,800	
J. T. Stoddard					4,800
Woods & Connell					7,000
A. Wentworth	140	24,000	20,000	2,557	
C. J. Bishop & Co.					85,000
Pierce & Fuller					5,000
T. & Mary Mason	136	22,000	18,000	2,562	14,700
Wilson & Kearney		22,000	18,000	2,587	
J. M. Roberts	132				2,000
Hewins & Gay					25,000
Ed. Turner					
H. D. Parker	130	22,000	18,000	2,550	2,000
Scribner & O'Brien					45,500
Buckinam, Raynor & Co.					25,500
H. B. Farwell & Co.					3,000
A. O. Burbank					
P. B. Brigham	126	22,000	18,000	2,550	10,000
E. H. Furber & Co.					6,900
Saunders Bros. & Co.					
S. Oliver, Jr.					500
P. B. Brigham		22,000	18,000	2,482	
J. H. Adden					10,000
A. E. Bridge & Co.					3,000

DETAILS OF LOSSES. 67

J. McGregor	118			
Jenkens, Lalle & Son		23,000	20,000	2,830	75,000
George J. Hopkins					4,000
Wm. Bramhall (estate)	114	22,000	18,000	2,548	3,800
Newton, Hartt & Co					15,000
Wallace & Macomber					
W. F. Weld	110	22,000	20,000	2,544	
Boyd, Cory, Ahe & Co					40,000
J. M. Jones	106	22,000	20,000	2,544	
E. A. Copen & Co					8,000
E. Mann & Son					20,000
J. M. Jones & Co					150,500
Clark, Kent & Co					15,000
Frederick Jones	102	22,000	20,000	2,544	
" " & Co					449,900
J. Osborn, Jr. & Co					4,000
J. P. Crane & Co	102				4,000
M. C. Ferris	94–92	48,000	32,000	3,000	

PEARL PLACE.

James Carboy (heirs)	14	$5,500	$3,000	1,138
Trustees Per. Peace Fund	13	5,000	3,000	1,142
Timothy McCarthy	12	5,000	3,000	1,146
P. McPhilomey	11	5,000	3,000	1,149
J. O'Keefe	10	5,000	3,000	1,161
Pat. M. Glarry	15	5,500	3,000	1,248
T. Lyons	16	3,500	3,000	791
Helen M. Hobbs	17	3,700	2,800	884

PEARL PLACE—*Continued.*

Names.	Nos.	Value of Land.	Value of Buildings.	Square Feet of Land.	Personal.
J. Wall	9	$3,500	$2,500	881	......
J. Quinn	8	3,500	3,000	1,161	......
"	7	4,500	3,000	1,159	$2,000
Tim. Cronan	6	5,000	3,500	1,149	......
Ada P. Morse	5	6,000	3,000	1,195	......
John Foster	4	6,000	3,000	1,184	......

PURCHASE STREET.

Names.	Nos.	Value of Land.	Value of Buildings.	Square Feet of Land.	Personal.
C. E. Cook	4	$15,000	$5,000	890	......
J. Frederick (heirs)	2	9,000	2,000	540	......
J. Milton Roberts	......	24,000	24,000	1,583	......
A. Strong et als	......	32,000	24,000	3,089	......
F. Shaw	9	60,000	40,000	6,241	......
Newhall & Tucker	......	......	......	......	$40,000
F. Shaw & Bro	......	......	......	......	25,000
H. L. Richardson (heirs)	15	36,000	2,000	3,900	......
J. Calfe	......	......	......	......	4,000
M. A. Ring	17	15,000	3,000	1,709	......
J. Quinn	......	......	......	......	2,000
T. Tileston (heirs)	19	15,000	2,000	1,650	......
Mary Tileston (heirs)	21	14,000	2,000	1,590	......
St. Stephen's Church	23	......	......	......	......

DETAILS OF LOSSES.

Episcopal City Mission	....	27,000	3,000	3,450
T. Remick et als	39	13,000	2,000	1,882
T. Remick	....	13,000	2,000	1,800
J. P. Preston	47	20,000	10,000	3,209
" "	57	20,000	10,000	2,614
E. B. Phillips	59	19,000	6,000	2,523
" "	67	19,000	6,000	3,013
C. Stetson et als	71	10,000	6,000	1,465
St. Vincent's Church	....	50,000	....	7,222
T. Tileston (heirs)	23	16,000	2,000	1,782

SOUTH STREET.

J. P. Cooke	3	$42,000	$3,000	3,000
S. Cohen	9	25,000	5,000	2,377
J. S. Stone	11	20,000	3,000	2,887
Wm. Sturgis (heirs)	13	18,000	4,000	2,392
M. L. Maynz	15	20,000	4,000	2,942
Alex. Fullerton	17	20,000	5,000	2,900
Michael Rothe	19	19,000	5,000	2,900
" "	4	13,000	4,000	2,260

STURGIS STREET.

H. F. Smith et als	10	$8,000	$4,000	1,125

SULLIVAN PLACE.

Names.	Nos.	Value of Land.	Value of Buildings.	Square Feet of Land.	Personal.
G. T. Bigelow et als.	5	$5,000	$2,000	1,140	......
Wright & Whitman.	6	5,000	2,000	1,140	......

SUMMER STREET.

Names.	Nos.	Value of Land.	Value of Buildings.	Square Feet of Land.	Personal.
J. C. Gray.	......	$250,000	$60,000	6,850	......
Wheeler & Wilson S. M. Co.	......	......	......	......	$15,000
V. Brandley & Co.	......	......	......	......	5,000
Webber & Twitchell.	......	......	......	......	500
Summer Street Club.	......	......	......	......	1,000
Clarendon Club.	......	......	......	......	300
Shreve, Crump & Low.	......	......	......	......	182,100
E. W. Miles.	11-13	47,000	12,000	2,250	......
Miles, Burr & Co.	......	......	......	......	28,600
R. C. Winthrop.	15-17	47,000	15,000	2,250	......
J. F. Stetson.	......	......	......	......	1,000
Moon, Pickering & Co.	......	......	......	......	30,000
S. Salisbury (heirs).	19	59,000	17,000	2,250	......
J. Leeds.	39-41	42,000	20,000	2,250	......
M. Walko & Co.	......	......	......	......	12,000
A. C. Hersey.	43-45	42,000	23,000	2,250	......
G. W. Carnes & Co.	......	......	......	......	30,000
W. N. Todd & Co.	......	......	......	......	30,000

DETAILS OF LOSSES. 71

Forbes, Richardson & Co.	47-49				$70,000
G. H. Kuhn (trustee)		100,000		4,450	
Howes & Monks	55-57	80,000	55,000	3,840	
Mitchell, Green & Stevens			70,000		85,000
A. Hardy et als. (trustees)	59	110,000		6,722	
Erving, Wise & Fuller			70,000		75,000
Wyman & Arkley	61				77,400
Srecker Bros	63				12,000
H. H. Peters	65-67	90,000		7,060	
S. Klous & Co.			70,000		76,000
Garvin & Howe					15,000
Jordan, Clark & Co.					125,000
Stiles, Beal & Homer					43,600
Morse, Hammond & Co.					35,000
J. Sleeper	71-73	42,000	30,000	2,674	
Charlotte A. Johnson	75-77	40,000	15,000	2,674	
G. H Butler					1,200
A. Folsom & Co.					60,000
P. Carney		64,000	20,000	3,095	
Smith, Richardson & Corson	79			5,021	65,000
G. M. Glazier					20,000
S. Klous	83-85	125,000	75,000		130,400
Tebbetts, Baldwin & D.					25,000
Damon, Temple & Co.					45,000
A. K. Young & Co.		49,000			100,000
J. C. Haynes	89-91		26,000	2,715	
Sawyer, Mansfield & Co.					40,000
Leland, Wheelock & Co.					
Rhoades & Kipley	93-95	49,000	26,000	2,880	65,000
Eager, Bartlett & Co.					

SUMMER STREET—Continued.

NAMES.	Nos.	Value of Land.	Value of Buildings.	Square Feet of Land.	Personal.
O. R. North & Son	......	......	......	......	25,000
H. H. Hunnewell (trustee)	97–99	$70,000	$60,000	5,789	......
Farley, Amsden & Co	......	......	......	......	60,400
Rhoades, Ripley & Co	......	......	......	......	154,100
R. H. Stearns	101–103	51,000	50,000	3,711	3,000
Minot, Hooper & Co	......	......	......	......	53,500
Sanderson, Foster & Co	......	......	......	......	
Faxon Bros	105–107	51,000	50,000	3,166	97,900
Beard, Moulton & Co	......	......	......	......	15,000
Faxon & Elms	109–111	70,000	50,000	2,904	50,000
N. E. Lithograph Co	......	......	......	......	
Hardy, Mayhew & Co	......	......	......	......	3,000
Wm. Boynton	115–117	45,000	35,000	2,400	8,000
G. A. Clark & Co	......	......	......	......	
Potter & Smith	......	......	......	......	30,000
Lucy A. Harris	119–121	30,000	24,000	2,300	20,000
S. Walker & Co	......	......	......	......	10,000
Farnum, Flagg & Co	......	......	......	......	
Myers & Knapp	......	......	......	......	
J. Cottle	123–125	38,000	37,000	3,161	22,000
J. S. Stone & Co	......	......	......	......	10,000
Rice & Hutchins	......	......	......	......	
J. N. Menzel	127	20,000	6,000	1,938	......
H. Allen (heirs)	129	20,000	6,000	1,950	......
F. M. Hartwell	131	13,000	4,000	1,200	......

DETAILS OF LOSSES.

Walter Baker (heirs)	42	50,000	25,000	2,413	......
Frederick Gleason	......	......	......	......	700
Marean & Co	......	......	......	......	3,000
Seavey, Foster & Bowman	......	......	......	......	50,000
Lewis, Brown & Co	......	......	......	......	50,000
Wm. Minot, Jr. (trustee)	46	48,000	15,000	2,600	......
Nicholson & Adams	......	......	......	......	10,000
Edgerton & Co	......	......	......	......	5,000
C. E. Wolcott	48	50,000	25,000	2,716	......
G. H. Lane, Brett & Co	......	......	......	......	72,900
E. F. Messenger & Co	......	......	......	......	12,400
Wm. Gray	52	115,000	100,000	5,763	......
C. E. King & Co	......	......	......	......	125,000
Cushing, Young & Co	......	......	......	......	1,000
Davis & Frost	......	......	......	......	5,000
C. O. Rogers (heirs)	58	68,000	52,000	4,226	......
Phillips, Sherman & Co	......	......	......	......	90,000
Wheil Bros. & Dreyfus	......	......	......	......	50,000
Faxon Bros	62	75,000	75,000	4,338	......
Marr Bros	......	......	......	......	45,000
D. Lyons & Co	......	......	......	......	65,000
Faxon Bros	68	127,000	103,000	6,070	......
Maffyn, Mullen & Elms	......	......	......	......	75,000
Conant Bros	......	......	......	......	16,000
H. A. Jenks & Co	......	......	......	......	6,000
Herman & Lautenbach	......	......	......	......	6,000
Bowen, Moore & Co	......	......	......	......	4,000
Harding Bros. & Co	......	......	......	......	12,000
Brainard, Davy & Co	......	......	......	......	15,000
Foster Waterman (lessee)	74	81,000	45,000	4,050	......

SUMMER STREET—*Continued.*

Names.	Nos.	Value of Land.	Value of Buildings.	Square Feet of Land.	Personal.
Wheelwright, Anderson & Co.	....	....	....	....	$175,000
Brown, Dutton & Co.	....	....	....	....	36,200
Leman Klous.	80	$70,000	$47,000	3,516	....
B. L. Solomon & Sons.	....	....	....	....	30,000
Louis & Cohen.	....	....	....	....	17,000
Jewett & Bush.	....	....	....	....	55,000
Perry, Cook & Tower.	....	....	....	....	65,000
J. W. Beals.	94–96	68,000	32,000	3,224	....
W. R. A. A. Lawrence et als.	139	26,000	9,000	2,001	....
Dwyer & Barrett.	....	....	....	....	5,000
Geo. W. Wales.	141	....	....	....	1,000
Wm. Jones.	....	....	....	....	3,000
Kinney, Gallagher & Co.	143	18,000	8,000	2,000	....
Wright Bros.	....	....	....	....	5,000
Samuel G. Reed.	145	15,000	15,000	1,912	....
White Bros. & Kilburn.	....	....	....	....	5,000
B. S. McIntosh & Co.	....	....	....	....	5,000
Elizabeth N. Fiske.	149	15,000	6,000	2,615	....
Ann F. Dawson.	151	12,000	6,000	1,786	....
John Quinn.	....	....	....	....	2,000
Ann F. Dawson.	153	12,000	6,000	1,716	....
S. F. Constant (heirs).	155	13,000	3,000	1,777	....
"	157	13,000	3,000	1,732	....
J. A. Preston.	159	11,500	3,000	1,558	....
"	163	10,500	3,000	1,425	....

DETAILS OF LOSSES. 75

Name	No.				
Patrick H. Spellman					600
Daniel S. Johnson	147			2,125	
J. H. & G. K. Thorndike	12–14	15,000	8,000	8,400	
Wm. P. Mason et als. (trustees)	24–36	150,000	70,000	26,718	
Stedman & Pember		375,000	100,000		38,000
C. C. Holbrook & Co	24				90,000
Clapp, Evans & Co	26				50,000
Barnum & Wright	28				12,000
W. B. Fowle (agent)	30				18,000
W. J. Schofield	32				1,000
Hecht Bros					2,000
Grover & Baker S. M. Co	34				100,000
Spinger Bros					8,300
McDewell & Adams	36				15,000
J. I. Bowditch	38	48,000	24,000	2,550	
Porter Bros. & Co					1,000
Boyce, Tuck & Co	40				35,000
Prager, Bock & Co					80,000
Leman Klous	84–86	83,000	60,000	3,952	
D. B. Saunders & Co	96				25,000
Claflin, Larrabee & Co					30,000
A. Dearborn et als	98	80,000	55,000	5,314	
Heyer Bros					102,500
H. C. Gilbert & Lovejoy	102				50,000
J. M. Bell		30,000	10,000	2,016	
Brigham, Jones & Co					12,000
John Cotter					10,000
Dexter, Follett (heirs)	108	32,000	10,000	2,608	
Amidon & Co					5,000
Hodkins & Barnard					10,000

SUMMER STREET—*Continued.*

Names.	Nos.	Value of Land.	Value of Buildings.	Square Feet of Land.	Personal.
J. H. Lee et als............	110	$35,000	$20,000	3,202	....
I. Collamore & Co.........	....	....	....	....	$25,200
I. H. Sears.................	....	....	....	....	18,000
Geo. H. Reed & Sons......	....	....	....	....	5,000
James Hyndman............	116	36,000	24,000	3,640	....
W. Fessenden..............	....	....	....	....	1,000
I. B. Brooks & Co.........	....	....	....	....	8,000
Davis Bros. & Winch......	....	....	....	....	8,000
Houghton & Bailey........	....	....	....	....	17,000
C. W. Thurston............	....	....	....	....	6,000
E. B. Phillips..............	122	41,000	25,000	4,127	....
Dunham & Whitney........	....	....	....	....	2,000
G. D. Vaughan & Co......	....	....	....	....	2,000
Whiteman, Whitcomb & Co.	....	....	....	....	2,000
F. S. Hill & Co............	....	....	....	....	5,000
E. B. Phillips..............	128	50,000	40,000	4,200	....
Rising, Thompson & Co...	....	....	....	....	43,600
Ames & Coburn............	....	....	....	....	14,300
J. Vaughan & Co...........	....	....	....	....	17,000
J. C. Currier & Co.........	....	....	....	....	500
Isaac Rich (heirs)..........	130	54,000	41,000	4,140	....
D. B. Stedman.............	....	....	....	....	75,500
Guilford White.............	138	12,000	3,000	944	....
Leonard Ware..............	140	8,500	2,500	700	....
"	142	7,500	2,500	643	....

DETAILS OF LOSSES.

T. Montgomery (heirs)	144	6,000	460	....
Cate & Nickerson	150	21,000	1,375	10,000
Geo. Lawton	152	50,000	3,277	....

WASHINGTON STREET.

Samuel Davis (heirs)	148	$40,000	525	$20,000
Currier, Trott & Co	....	....	....	50,300
H. W. Dutton & Son	150	90,000	2,185	....
T. H. Swett (heirs)	154	72,000	1,871	12,800
John Earle & Co	....	....	....	22,300
Davis, Roundy & Co	....	....	....	....
P. Parker et als. (trustees)	156	60,000	1,900	65,000
Kelly & Edmands	....	....	....	18,000
H. T. Shear & Son	....	....	....	....
C. F. Shimmin et als	158	100,000	4,000	75,000
J. W. Plympton & Co	....	....	....	16,200
Wm. White & Co	....	....	....	....
J. Parker	160–162	97,000	3,879	205,300
Palmer & Batchelder	....	....	....	30,000
D. C. Percival, Jr. & Co	....	....	....	3,000
H. A. Forbes (agent)	....	....	....	6,000
W. G. Watson & Son	....	....	....	2,000
Benj. A. Hersey	....	....	....	....
C. B. & A. Whiting	164	90,000	3,130	....
Fowle, Torry & Co	....	....	....	90,000
W. B. Callender (heirs)	166–168	133,000	6,383	....
Bruce, Whitney & Co	....	....	....	20,000
J. D. Barber	....	....	....	4,000

WASHINGTON STREET—Continued.

Names.	Nos.	Value of Land.	Value of Buildings.	Square Feet of Land.	Personal.
J. A. Lowell (trustee)	170	$120,000	$55,000	4,380	....
Jameson & Clarke	....	....	....	....	$20,000
Weeks & Potter	....	....	....	....	200,000
W. S. Dexter et als. (trustees)	172	75,000	15,000	2,600	....
E. Hixon & Co	....	....	....	....	20,000
T. B. Williams	174	56,000	30,000	1,870	....
Carpenter, Plimpton & Co	....	....	....	....	25,500
M. Williams	176–178	53,000	30,000	1,870	....
Bradford & Anthony	....	....	....	....	92,400
J. A. Lowell (trustee)	180–182	84,000	60,000	2,400	....
Call & Tuttle	....	....	....	....	50,000
W. H. Slocum	....	....	....	....	52,500
J. C. Chaffin	186	70,000	50,000	2,000	....
Russell & Richardson	....	....	....	....	2,000
J. C. Chaffin & Co	....	....	....	....	25,000
J. Collamore	188–190	76,000	34,000	2,600	....
Jacobs & Deane	....	....	....	....	21,000
Fiske, Tomlinson & Co	....	....	....	....	10,000
Henry Sargent (heirs)	192	142,000	30,000	7,600	....
J. H. Pray Sons & Co	....	....	....	....	300,000
A. Hardy et als. (trustees)	194–200	220,000	140,000	11,948	....
Macullar, Williams & Parker	....	....	....	....	250,000
G. Howe (heirs)	202–208	142,000	23,000	5,300	....
Copeland & Co	....	....	....	....	8,000
Wm. Bogle	....	....	....	....	1,500

DETAILS OF LOSSES.

Ann W. Giles................	210–212	38,000	8,000	1,237	......
Hobbs Bros..................	......	......	......	......	15,000
W. A. Hardwell.............	......	......	......	......	300
J. Richardson...............	214–216	50,000	10,000	1,635	......
W. H. Allen.................	......	......	......	......	20,000
J. H. Sassard...............	......	......	......	......	1,500
Chas. L. Woodbury..........	......	......	......	......	22,000
D. L. Gibbens (heirs).......	218	47,000	10,000	1,570	......
Solomon Sibley.............	......	......	......	......	1,000
L. Newman & Co............	......	......	......	......	3,000
M. Williams, Jr. (trustee)...	230–222	75,000	12,000	2,550	......
Fowler & Jacobs............	......	......	......	......	3,000
J. Frank Miles..............	......	......	......	......	8,500

WATER STREET.

Geo. D. Howe et als. (trustees)...	60–72	$125,000	$50,000	4,300	......
C. Woodberry & Sons........	......	......	......	......	$1,000
Kennerick & Peirce..........	......	......	......	......	500
A. Clarkson.................	......	......	......	......	800
H. M. Wiswell...............	......	......	......	......	500
Mears, Stetson & Co........	......	......	......	......	1,000
J. H. Symonds..............	......	......	......	1,895	2,000
J. M. Codman...............	80	40,000	20,000	......	......
Averill & Huntley...........	......	......	......	......	10,000
J. M. Cushing...............	......	......	......	......	500
B. F. Allen..................	......	......	......	......	10,000
G. H. Merrill................	......	......	......	......	1,000

WATER STREET—*Continued.*

Names.	Nos.	Value of Land.	Value of Buildings.	Square Feet of Land.	Personal.
Eichom Bros............	....	....	....	....	$5,300
Peirson Bros. & Co......	....	....	....	....	33,300
Small & Appleton.......	....	....	....	....	4,000
C. W. Codman (heirs)...	Kilby & Water	$98,000	$14,000	3,500	....
Moses Williams.........	101	35,000	12,000	1,500	....
J. Porter & Co..........	....	....	....	....	5,000
Merchants Insurance Co.	45–57	180,000	70,000	7,300	11,000
A. M. Sweet............	....	....	....	....	4,000
A. W. Lock & Co........	....	....	....	....	500
Stand, Stanley & Co.....	....	....	....	....	1,000
J. D. Flagg & Co........	....	....	....	....	1,000
C. P. Stevens...........	67–69	32,000	8,000	970	....
J. C. Howe & J. J. French.	....	....	....	....	15,000
A. Wheeler (agent)......	71–73	35,000	10,000	1,600	....
J. C. Howe & J. J. French.	....	....	....	....	10,000
Dexter Bryant..........	75–77	25,000	9,000	1,500	....
J. P. Cushing (heirs)....	77–81	21,000	7,000	1,400	....
" " "	83–85	21,000	7,000	1,400	....
" " "	87–89	21,000	7,000	1,500	....
Rogers & Sheldon.......	....	....	....	....	20,000
Dudley & Wood.........	....	....	....	....	1,000
C. Dean (trustee).......	91–93	18,000	7,000	1,054	....
Wm. Page & Son........	....	....	....	....	25,000
J. P. Cook.............	95–97	20,000	5,000	1,300	....

G. H. Hood (agent)	......	......	......	1,000
David Hinckley (heirs)	98	32,000	8,000	950	......
Wm. Crosby	......	......	......	......	6,000
Treasurer Tufts Coll	......	22,000	8,000	1,000	......

WINTHROP SQUARE.

J. M. Beebe	1–3	$175,000	$125,000	11,050	......
Haughton, Perkins, Woods & Co	......	......	......	......	$308,400
A. T. Stewart & Co	3	......	......	......	150,000
Wm. F. Weld	4–56	140,000	110,000	6,782	......
Parker, Wilder & Co	......	......	......	......	156,700
Anderson, Heath & Co	......	......	......	......	300,000
Josiah Bardwell	19–21	28,000	20,000	1,131	......
Marshall & Cutter	......	......	......	......	7,500

RECAPITULATION.

Streets.	Value of Land.	Value of Buildings.	Personal.	Square Feet of Land.
Arch	$136,000	$78,000	$191,800	9,995
Bath	51,000	19,000	15,300	4,500
Broad	1,040,000	116,000	295,000	391,129
Bussey Place	30,500	20,500	5,000	5,345
Channing	32,000	11,000	10,000	3,910
Columbia	100,000	24,500	....	8,560
Congress	2,086,000	1,230,000	3,009,900	176,135
Devonshire	1,051,000	575,000	2,561,800	55,880
Federal	2,402,000	1,356,000	3,367,300	208,801
Federal Court	30,000	3,000	....	6,510
Franklin	2,222,000	1,401,000	5,841,600	111,355
Gridley	17,000	9,000	....	3,456
Hawes	5,000	500	....	500
Hawley	174,000	73,000	54,000	16,644
High	1,389,500	1,021,000	3,326,100	118,514
Kilby	554,000	195,500	1,243,400	27,473
Leather Square	10,000	4,000	....	2,500
Lincoln	37,000	45,000	8,500	5,069
Lindall	154,000	68,000	53,500	12,057
Matthew	36,500	46,500	40,000	6,012
Merchants' Exchange	450,000	100,000	....	1,700
Milk	1,991,000	910,000	2,944,600	103,144
Milton Place	69,000	36,000	10,000	15,230
Morton Place	64,000	45,000	14,900	14,680
Oliver	126,000	87,000	150,000	12,358
Otis	339,000	216,000	1,056,500	19,720
Pearl	2,466,000	1,531,000	7,251,800	218,590
Pearl Place	66,700	41,800	2,000	15,388
Purchase	427,000	153,000	71,000	50,152
South	177,000	33,000	....	21,658
Sturgis	8,000	4,000	....	1,125
Sullivan Place	10,000	4,000	....	2,280
Summer	3,616,000	2,023,000	4,042,700	225,590
Washington	1,930,000	766,000	1,794,100	73,433
Water	725,000	242,000	170,400	31,169
Winthrop Square	343,000	255,000	922,600	18,963
Total	$24,365,200	$12,745,300	$38,453,800	1,999,525

RECAPITULATION.

There were **1,999,525** feet of land burned over. The value of this land was **$24,365,200**. The assessed valuation of the buildings burnt was **$12,745,300**; the assessors estimated they were assessed within ten per cent. of their valuation; adding this, would make their real valuation **$14,019,830**. The personal property was assessed at **$38,453,800**. This was supposed by the assessors to represent two thirds of its valuation. Adding one third, would make **$51,271,700**. The estimated value of consigned goods destroyed was **$10,000,000**, making the total loss by the fire about **$75,291,530**; **552** separate estates and **999** firms were burned out. The valuation of Boston was **$682,724,300**, hence the loss was about a tenth part of the whole. The increase the last year was **$70,060,750**, hence the loss was about the same as the annual increase.

INSURANCE LOSSES.

A belief in the indestructibility of Boston's granite warehouses; a feeling of pride and confidence in her fire department, which had never before been defeated; and the peculiar character of the mutual system upon which most of her buildings were insured, only allowing three-fourths of the value to be covered,—all tended to prevent a proper amount of insurance; and as so large a proportion of that which existed was in Boston offices, the loss fell with accumulated force upon her own citizens.

The annihilation of capital invested in insurance stocks, and the assessments required by the mutual companies, must be added to the loss on buildings, stocks, rents, and interruption to business, in obtaining an accurate estimate of the disaster.

We are indebted to Mr. Charles H. Frothingham, 16 Devonshire street, Boston, for the following statistics of the insurance losses; and every exertion has been made to have the list as accurate as possible at the time of going to press.

JOINT-STOCK COMPANIES DOING BUSINESS IN BOSTON.

Companies.	Capital.	Assets.	Losses in Boston.	Will pay.
American, Boston............	$300,000	$946,030	$456,117	All.
Bay State, Worcester.........	200,000	325,000	280,000	50 p. c.
Boston, Boston...............	300,000	600,000	1,320,000	40 "
Boylston, Boston.............	300,000	912,000	1,800,000	56 "
City, Boston.................	200,000	375,561	800,000	40 "
Eliot, Boston................	300,000	684,817	1,700,000	35 "
Exchange, Boston.............	200,000	265,617	775,000	40 "
Faneuil Hall, Boston.........	200,000	250,000	600,000	35 "
Firemen's, Boston............	300,000	1,000,000	2,800,000	30 "
First National, Worcester....	100,000	175,000	50,000	All.
Franklin, Boston.............	300,000	731,486	2,000,000	25 p. c.
Gloucester, Gloucester.......	100,000	117,852	27,000	All.
Howard, Boston...............	200,000	385,000	1,000,000	25 p. c.
Lawrence, Boston.............	250,000	299,940	500,000	35 "
Manufacturers', Boston.......	400,000	1,500,000	1,700,000	90 "
Mercantile Marine............	300,000	550,000	133,000	All.
Merchants', Boston...........	500,000	1,034,004	2,844,354	30 p. c.
Mutual Benefit, Boston.......	200,000	281,603	995,000	35 "
National, Boston.............	300,000	896,681	950,000	40 "
Neptune, Boston..............	300,000	896,633	2,200,000	40 "
North American, Boston.......	200,000	651,488	1,200,000	50 "
People's, Worcester..........	400,000	800,293	650,000	60 "
Prescott, Boston.............	200,000	508,189	700,000	50 "
Shoe and Leather, Boston.....	200,000	593,754	1,900,000	30 "
Springfield, Springfield.....	500,000	1,055,106	250,000	All.
Suffolk, Boston..............	150,000	275,717	645,000	35 p. c.
Traders and Mechanics', Lowell	100,000	208,847		All.
Tremont, Boston..............	200,000	267,000	750,000	34 p. c.
Washington, Boston...........	300,000	1,070,743	1,096,700	75 "

MASSACHUSETTS MUTUAL COMPANIES.

Companies.	Capital.	Assets.	Losses in Boston.	Will pay.
Central, Worcester...........	......	$31,850	$10,000	All.
Dorchester, Boston...........	......	159,000	134,130	"
Essex, Salem.................	......	90,000	22,500	"
Holyoke, Salem...............	......	338,496	220,650	"
India Mutual, Boston,........	......	697,184	380,000	"
Massachusetts, Boston........	......	750,000	1,200,000	99 p. c.
Mechanics', Boston...........	......	2,000,000	1,331,401	All.
Merchants' and Farmers', Worcester	......	850,000	300,000	"
Naumkeag, Salem..............	......	3,173	2,800	"
New England, Boston..........	......	513,000	200,000	"
Quincy, Quincy...............	......	480,000	432,500	"
Salem........................	......	100,000	59,000	"
Union, Boston................	......	900,000	1,200,000	75 p. c.
Cambridge....................	......	132,500	25,250	All.

COMPANIES OF OTHER STATES DOING BUSINESS IN BOSTON.

Companies.	Capital.	Assets.	Losses in Boston.	Will pay.
Adriatic, New York..............	$200,000	$216,250	$7,500	All.
Allemania, Cleveland...............	250,000	304,027	5,000	"
Alps, Erie.....	250,000	340,687	34,000	"
Amazon, Cincinnati................	500,000	850,000	20,000	"
American Central, St. Louis........ ...	275,000	365,161	15,000	"
American Exchange, New York.....	200,000	225,491	10,000	"
American, New York...............	400,000	1,000,500	75,000	"
American, Philadelphia.............	400,000	1,133,593	500,000	"
Arctic, New York..................	250,000	349,877	100,000	"
Atlantic, Brooklyn.................	200,000	200,000	25,500	"
Atlantic, Providence................	......	......	24,000	"
Ætna, Hartford.....................	3,000,000	6,400,502	1,300,000	"
Ætna, New York...................	200,000	202,493	40,000	"
Bangor, Bangor.....................	......	300,000	50,000	"
Black River, Watertown............	250,000	250,000	85,000	"
Brewers', Milwaukee...............	200,000	377,918	55,500	"
Brewers and Maltsters', New York..	350,000	260,796	75,000	"
Capital, New York.................	200,000	125,000	2,000	"
Capital City, Albany...............	150,000	177,142	24,000	"
Citizens, New York................	300,000	780,793	250,000	"
City, New York....................	210,000	500,523	90,000	"
City, Providence......................	100,000	172,150	10,000	"
Clinton, New York.................	250,000	441,339	95,000	"
Columbia, New York...............	300,000	467,198	104,000	"
Commerce, Albany.................	200,000	420,203	50,000	"
Commerce, New York	200,000	253,146	62,000	"
Commercial, New York............	200,000	335,982	100,000	"
Connecticut, Hartford..............	500,000	500,363	100,000	"
Continental, New York.	1,000,000	2,509,526	460,000	"
Corn Exchange, New York.........	200,000	309,936	140,000	"
Delaware Mutual Safety, Philadel...	360,000	202,255	375,000	"
Eastern, Bangor....................	225,000	335,000	180,000	"
Empire City, New York............	200,000	280,000	10,000	"
Equitable, New York...............	210,000	460,000	20,000	"
Equitable, Providence..............	200,000	430,000	314,800	"
Exchange, New York.........	150,000	282,221	15,000	"
Fame, Philadelphia................	200,000	217,614	20,600	"
Fairfield County, Connecticut........	200,000	275,000	70,000	"
Farmers, New York.......	100,000	189,219	5,000	"
Farragut, New York................	......	139,219	20,000	"
Firemen's, New York...............	204,000	340,616	122,000	"
Firemen's Fund, San Francisco.....	500,000	856,788	70,000	"
Firemen's Trust, New York........	150,000	242,255	5,000	"
Franklin, Philadelphia..............	400,000	3,255,749	420,000	"
Gebhard, New York................	200,000	250,667	22,500	"
Germania, New York..............	500,000	1,033,602	400,000	"

THE BOSTON FIRE.

Companies.	Capital.	Assets.	Losses in Boston.	Will pay.
Globe, New York..................	$200,000	$327,748	$15,000	All.
German, Erie......................	200,000	237,083	50,000	"
German American, New York.......	1,000,000	1,000,000	109,000	"
Girard, Philadelphia...............	300,000	571,423	50,000	"
Glens Falls, New York.............	200,000	577,312	50,000	"
Greenwich, New York..............	......	......	20,000	"
Guardian, New York........	200,000	266,155	50,000	"
Hanover, New York...............	400,000	950,000	225,000	"
Hartford, Connecticut.............	1,000,000	2,942,061	522,000	"
Hoffman, New York...............	200,000	299,741	100,000	"
Home, New York..................	2,500,000	4,672,044	100,000	"
Home, Columbus..................	500,000	871,453	40,000	"
Hope, New York...................	150,000	203,101	50,000	"
Humboldt.........................	200,000	304,090	230,000	60 p. c.
Ins. Co. N. A., Philadelphia........	500,000	3,212,176	900,000	All.
Ins. Co. St. Penn., Philadelphia.....	200,000	447,934	75,000	"
Irving, New York	200,000	250,000	105,500	"
International, New York...........	500,000	1,065,113	417,000	75 p. c.
Importers and Traders', New York..	200,000	295,850	32,000	All.
Jefferson, New York...............	200,000	415,919	10,000	"
King's County, New York..........	150,000	249,758	5,000	"
Lafayette, New York.........	150,000	211,789	5,000	"
Lamar, New York.................	200,000	252,000	104,000	"
Lenox, New York.................	100,000	200,000	18,000	"
Lorillard, New York...............	300,000	300,000	92,000	"
Lycoming, Muncy, Pa..............	......	......	10,000	"
Manhattan, New York.............	250,000	260,000	54,000	"
Market, New York.................	200,000	200,000	100,000	"
Mechanics and Traders', New York.	200,000	474,758	25,000	"
Mercantile, New York.............	200,000	293,294	68,800	"
Meriden, Conn...	200,000	240,000	33,000	"
Merchants', Providence............	200,000	380,982	210,000	"
Montauk, New York...............	150,000	297,407	5,000	"
Merchants', New York.............	200,000	475,088	126,500	"
Narragansett, Providence.....	500,000	773,823	300,000	"
National, Bangor..................	200,000	449,560	......	75 p. c.
National, Philadelphia.............	200,000	300,000	25,000	All.
National, Hartford................	500,000	517,205	115,000	"
National, New York...............	200,000	297,468	140,000	"
New Hampshire, Manchester.......	100,000	150,174	10,000	"
New York and Yonkers............	200,000	200,000	70,000	"
Niagara, New York.............. ..	1,000,000	1,256,240	366,000	"
Orient, Connecticut...............	500,000	575,761	170,000	"
Pacific, New York.................	200,000	468,324	15,000	"
Penn, Philadelphia............. ...	152,600	161,370	5,000	"
Pennsylvania, Philadelphia.........	400,000	1,257,554	500,000	"
Penn. Underwriters', Philadelphia...	200,000	......	15,000	"
Phenix, Brooklyn.................	1,000,000	1,827,660	450,000	"
Phœnix, Connecticut..............	600,000	1,908,831	500,000	"
Relief, New York..................	200,000	325,033	45,000	"

INSURANCE LOSSES.

Companies.	Capital.	Assets.	Losses in Boston.	Will pay.
Republic, New York................	$300,000	$503.774	$200,000	All.
Safeguard, New York...	200,000	240,000	15,000	"
Standard, New York...............	200,000	453,180	357,000	"
Star, New York................	200,000	372,326	150,000	"
St. Nicholas, New York...	150,000	239,494	15,000	"
St. Paul's F. and M., St. Paul......	400,000	532,629	20,000	"
State, Philadelphia................	......	......	5,000	"
State, Hannibal, Missouri..........	......	......	10,000	"
Traders', Chicago.................	500,000	600,000	60,000	"
Tradesmen's, New York...........	150,000	435,000	240,000	"
Triumph, Cincinnati...............	500,000	850,000	50,000	"
Union, Bangor.....................	200,000	540,785	150,000	"
Union, San Francisco..............	750,000	1,039,015	90,000	"
Union Mutual, Philadelphia........	139,820	259,725	34,500	"
United States, New York...........	250,000	......	5,000	"
Washington, New York............	200,000	213,061	50,000	50 p. c.
Washington, Providence...........	200,000	203,062	......	All.
Westchester, New York.	200,000	700,000	100,000	"
Williamsburgh City, New York.....	200,000	550,673	184,700	"

FOREIGN COMPANIES DOING BUSINESS IN BOSTON.

Companies.	Capital.	Assets, Jan. 1, 1871.	Losses.
Commercial Union, England........	$1,250,000	$12,000,000	$300,000
Hamburg..........................	....	1,000,000	45,000
Imperial, England.................	3,500,000	5,702,652	880,000
Liverpool and London and Globe....	1,956,760	20,106,900	1,731,500
London Assurance Corporation......	....	15,220,000	104,000
Lancashire, England...............	10,000,000	12,500,000	125,000
North British and Mercantile.......	1,250,000	5,410,333	600,000
Queen, England...	899,000	2,400,361	400,000
Royal, England....................	1,445,475	10,109,293	1,200,000

The following table shows the date of organization and the average annual dividend of the bankrupt insurance companies in this city:

Companies.	When organized.	Av. ann. Div'nd.
Boston..	1823	.11
Boylston..	1825	.14
City...	1850	.08
Eliot..	1851	.12
Faneuil Hall..	1871	.00
Firemen's...	1831	.15

Companies.	When organized.	Av. ann. Div'nd.
Franklin	1823	.09
Howard	1856	.10
Lawrence	1870	.00
Manufacturers'	1822	.17
Mercantile	1823	.10
Merchants'	1810	.19
National	1832	.15
Neptune	1831	.16
North American	1851	.11
Prescott	1856	.07
Shoe and Leather	1855	.10
Suffolk	1859	.05
Tremont	1867	.05
Washington	1826	.11

APPENDIX.

APPENDIX.

COMMONWEALTH OF MASSACHUSETTS.

In the Year One Thousand Eight Hundred and Seventy-Two.

AN ACT

To enable the City of Boston to make and issue its bonds for certain purposes.

Be it enacted by the Senate and House of Representatives, in General Court assembled, and by the authority of the same, as follows:

SECTION 1. The city of Boston is hereby authorized to make and issue its bonds for the purposes hereinafter set forth, payable to order, or bearer, in not more than fifteen years from date, for an amount not exceeding twenty millions of dollars, bearing an interest of not more than five per cent. per annum for those payable principal and interest in gold coin, and not more than six per cent. per annum for those payable principal and interest in legal-tender notes.

SECT. 2. A board of commissioners, of three persons, citizens of said Boston, shall be appointed by the mayor of said city, with the approval of the board of aldermen thereof, each of whom shall give bond with sureties to said city, in such sum as shall be fixed by the board of aldermen thereof, conditioned for the faithful discharge of his duty as commissioner; said commissioners shall receive such compensation for their services as shall be fixed by the city council, to be paid by said city.

SECT. 3. The duties and powers of said commissioners shall be as follows: they are hereby authorized to loan, in a safe and judicious manner, the proceeds of the bonds hereby authorized to be issued, in such sums as they shall determine, to the owners of land, the buildings upon which were burned by the fire in said Boston, on the ninth and tenth days of November, in the year eighteen hundred and seventy-two, upon the notes or bonds of such owners, secured by first mortgages of said land, said mortgages to be conditioned that the rebuilding shall be commenced within one year from the first day of January, in the year eighteen hundred and seventy-three, and said commissioners to have full power to apply the proceeds of said bonds in making said loans in such manner, and to make such further provisions, conditions, and limitations in reference to said loans, and securing the same, as shall be best calculated, in their judgment, to insure the employment of the same in rebuilding upon said land burned over, and the payment thereof to the said city. The loans upon such mortgages shall be payable in not more than ten years from date, and at a rate of interest of seven per centum per annum, payable semi-annually. When said loans are made, and the mortgages to secure them are completed, the said mortgages, notes, bonds, and securities connected therewith, are to be delivered by said commissioners to the treasurer of the city of Boston. The bonds hereby mentioned are to be negotiated and sold by and under the direction of said commissioners; but all proceeds received from such negotiation and sale are to be paid to the treasurer of said city. Said commissioners shall have authority to withhold the payment of any portion of a loan agreed to be made to an owner of land burned over by said fire, when it shall be necessary in their judgment so to do, to insure the speedy rebuilding on said land.

SECT. 4. A sinking fund shall be established for the payment of the bonds issued under this act, which shall consist of all premiums from the sale of said bonds above their par value, of all receipts of interest upon loans made under the authority of this act, over and above the interest paid on said bonds, and of all payments of the loans made under the authority of this act. The city treasurer shall keep an account of all sums received for said sinking fund, and the same shall be invested from time to time under the direction and authority of the commissioners of the sinking fund of the city of Boston; and the receipts of income from the sums so invested shall be held as a part of said fund, and be re-invested in the same manner as the principal. [And said commissioners of said sinking fund are authorized to invest any part thereof, in buying and cancelling the bonds issued by virtue of this act.] And when the bonds of said city, authorized by this act, become due and payable, said sinking fund shall be used and applied to the payment thereof.

Sect. 5. Vacancies in said board of commissioners shall be filled by the remaining commissioner or commissioners and the mayor of said city. And upon all matters that come before said board, they are to act by a majority of the board. Said commissioners, or any of them, may be removed from office by the supreme judicial court in their discretion, upon complaint of the mayor of said city, or of any ten citizens thereof, being tax payers, and said court is hereby empowered to adjudicate upon said complaint according to the course of proceedings in equity, and to make all proper decrees touching the same. If, from any cause, there shall be at any time vacancies in the whole of said board of commissioners, then new commissioners are to be appointed, as is hereinbefore provided for first filling said board.

Sect. 6. The treasurer of the city of Boston shall have the custody of all money received from the sale of the bonds hereby authorized, of all notes, bonds, mortgages, and securities taken by said commissioners, and of all money paid thereon, and of all money and securities belonging to said sinking fund, and shall give bond to said city with sureties for the faithful discharge of his duties under this act, to the satisfaction of the mayor of said city; and shall receive such compensation for his duties under this act as shall be determined by the city council of said city. He shall pay out the proceeds of the bonds sold to the persons to whom loans have been made under this act by said commissioners, upon the warrant of said commissioners signed by a majority of the board. He shall keep a separate account of all sums received and paid out under this act, and in the execution thereof, and also of the receipts and payments on account of said sinking fund, and of its condition, which accounts shall at all times be open to the inspection of the committee on finance and the city council of said city; and he shall, at the end of each half year, make a full report of his doings under this act, to the city council of said city, which shall be published in the newspapers in which the ordinances of the city are published.

Sect. 7. The said commissioners shall keep a true and careful record of all their doings under this act, also of the loans made, and the mortgages taken by them; and for this purpose they are authorized to appoint a clerk, whose compensation shall be fixed by the city council, and paid by said city. And said record shall at all times be open to the inspection of the committee on finance and of the city council of said city. And the commissioners shall at the end of each quarter make a full report of their doings to the city council, which shall be published in the newspapers in which the ordinances of the city are published.

SECT. 8. No loan under this act shall be made by said commissioners after one year from the first day of January, in the year 1873; but this shall not prevent the carrying into execution any contract for a loan under this act made by said commissioners before the expiration of said year, although the whole of said loan may not have been paid to the borrower before the expiration of said year.

SECT. 9. This act shall take effect upon its passage, but no action shall be taken under its provisions until it has been accepted by the city council of said city.

COMMONWEALTH OF MASSACHUSETTS.

CHAPTER 375.

AN ACT

To authorize the formation of Insurance companies, and for other purposes.

Be it enacted by the Senate and House of Representatives in General Court assembled, and by the authority of the same, as follows

SECTION 1. Any ten or more persons residents of this Commonwealth, who shall have associated themselves together by an agreement, in writing, such as is hereinafter described, with the intention to constitute a corporation for the purpose of transacting the business of insurance, either upon the stock or mutual principle, against loss or damage by fire, by lightning, by tempest, or by the perils of the sea, and other perils usually insured against by marine insurance companies, including risks of inland navigation and transportation, shall become a corporation upon complying with the provisions of section nine of this act, and shall remain a corporation, with all the powers, rights, and privileges, and subject to all the duties, liabilities, and restrictions set forth in all general laws which are or may be in force relating to insurance corporations.

SECT. 2. Such agreement shall set forth the fact that the subscribers thereto associate themselves with the intention to constitute a corporation, the name by which the corporation shall be known, the class or classes of insurance for the transaction of which the corporation is constituted, the plan or principle upon which the business is to be conducted, the town or city, which town or city shall be within this Commonwealth, in which it is established or located, and if a joint-stock company, the amount of its capital stock, and if a mutual company, with a guarantee capital, the amount thereof. The capital stock of a joint-stock company insuring against loss or damage by fire, or by fire and lightning only, shall not be less than two hundred thousand dollars if the company is located in Boston, and not less than one hundred thousand dollars if located elsewhere. If insuring marine or inland risks, either alone or in conjunction with fire risks, its capital stock shall not be less than three hundred thousand dollars if the company is located in Boston, and not less than two hundred thousand dollars if located elsewhere.

SECT. 3. Any mutual fire insurance company may be organized under the provisions of this act with a guarantee capital of not less than one hundred thousand dollars, and not more than three hundred thousand dollars, divided into shares of one hundred dollars each, and no policy shall be issued by such corporation until the whole amount of the guarantee capital fixed by the articles of association has been paid in in cash, and invested in accordance with the provisions of section thirty-one of chapter fifty-eight of the General Statutes, and chapter twenty-nine of the acts of the year eighteen hundred and sixty-four.

SECT. 4. Any mutual marine and mutual fire and marine insurance company may be organized under the provisions of this act, with a permanent fund of not less than four hundred thousand dollars, subscribed under the provisions of sections thirty-five and thirty-seven of chapter fifty-eight of the General Statutes; and no policy shall be issued by such corporation until one half said permanent fund has been paid in in cash, which shall be divided into shares of one hundred dollars each. Such corporations may increase said permanent fund to an amount not exceeding one million of dollars.

SECT. 5. Any name, not previously in use by any existing corporation or company, may be adopted: *provided*, that the words "*insurance company*" shall constitute a part of the title; and if the business is to be conducted upon the mutual principle, the words "*mutual* insurance company" shall constitute a part of such title. No certificate shall be granted to any corporation as hereinafter provided, if, in the judgment of the insurance commissioner, the name adopted too closely resembles the name of an existing corporation or company, or is likely to mislead the public.

Sect. 6. The first meeting for the purpose of organization shall be called by a notice, signed by one or more of the subscribers to such agreement, stating the time, place, and purpose of the meeting, a copy of which notice shall, seven days at least before the day appointed, be given to each subscriber, or left at his usual place of business or residence, or deposited in the post-office, postage prepaid, and addressed to him at his usual place of business or residence. And whoever gives such notices shall make affidavit of his doings, which shall be entered upon the records of the company: *provided, however,* that when organizations shall be commenced prior to the first day of January, in the year eighteen hundred and seventy-three, the foregoing notice may be waived by a written acknowledgment of the receipt of notice signed by the subscribers, which shall be sufficient evidence that due notice has been given.

Sect. 7. At such first meeting, including any adjournment thereof, an organization shall be effected by the choice by ballot of a temporary clerk, who shall be sworn to the faithful discharge of his duty, by the adoption of by-laws and by the election, in the manner provided by law, of directors and such other officers as the by-laws require; but at such first meeting no person shall be elected director who has not subscribed to the articles of association. The temporary clerk shall record the proceedings until and including the qualification of the secretary of the corporation by his being duly sworn.

Sect. 8. The directors so chosen shall elect a president, a secretary, and any other officers which under the by-laws they are authorized to choose.

Sect. 9. The president, secretary, and a majority of the directors shall forthwith make, sign, and swear to a certificate setting forth a copy of the articles of association, with the names of the subscribers thereto, the date of the first meeting, and of any adjournments thereof, and shall submit such certificate and the records of the corporation to the inspection of the insurance commissioner, who shall examine the same, and who may require such other evidence as he may judge necessary. The commissioner, if it shall appear that the requirements of the preceding sections of this act have been complied with, shall certify that fact, and his approval of the certificate, by indorsement thereon. Such certificate shall thereupon be filed in the office of the secretary of the Commonwealth by said officers, and upon being paid by them the fee hereinafter provided, the secretary shall cause the same, with the indorsement thereon, to be recorded, and shall thereupon issue to said corporation a certificate in the following form:

COMMONWEALTH OF MASSACHUSETTS.

Be it known, that whereas [here the names of subscribers to the articles of association shall be inserted], have associated themselves with the intention of forming a corporation under the name of [here the name of the corporation shall be inserted], for the purpose [here the purpose declared in the articles of association shall be inserted], with a capital or with a permanent fund of [here amount of capital or permanent fund fixed in the articles of association shall be inserted], and have complied with the provisions of the statutes of this Commonwealth in such case made and provided, as appears from the certificate of the president, secretary, and directors of said corporation, duly approved by the insurance commissioner, and recorded in this office. Now, therefore, I [here the name of the secretary shall be inserted], secretary of the Commonwealth of Massachusetts, do hereby certify that said [here the names of the subscribers to the articles of association shall be inserted], their associates and successors, are legally organized and established as, and are hereby made an existing corporation under the name of [here the name of the corporation shall be inserted], with the powers, rights, and privileges, and subject to the duties, liabilities, and restrictions which by law appertain thereto. Witness my official signature hereunto subscribed, and the seal of the Commonwealth of Massachusetts hereunto affixed this   day of   , in the year of our Lord   . [In these blanks the day, month, and year of execution of the certificate shall be inserted, and in the case of purely mutual companies, so much as relates to capital stock shall be omitted.]

The secretary of the Commonwealth shall sign the same, and cause the seal of the Commonwealth to be thereto affixed, and such certificate shall have the force and effect of a special charter, and be conclusive evidence of the organization and establishment of such corporation. The secretary shall also cause a record of such certificate to be made, and a copy of such record, duly certified, may, with like effect as the original certificate, be given in evidence, to prove the organization and establishment of such corporation.

SECT. 10. No policy shall be issued by a purely mutual company organized under the provisions of this act, until the sum of five hundred thousand dollars shall have been subscribed to be insured and entered on the books of the company: *provided, however*, that in any town of less than four thousand inhabitants, a company may be organized under the provisions of this act, to insure dwelling-houses, farm buildings, and contents only, within the limits of the town where said company is located, and may issue policies when fifty thousand dollars have been subscribed to be insured.

SECT. 11. The holders of stock in mutual fire insurance companies with a guarantee capital, organized under the provisions of this act, shall be entitled to a net semi-annual dividend not exceeding six per cent. on their respective shares, if the net profit, after providing for all expenses, losses, and liabilities then incurred, including a sum sufficient to reinsure all outstanding risks, is sufficient from time to time to pay the same; and if any such dividend is less than six per cent., it shall be made up when such net profit becomes sufficient therefor. Three fourths of said net profit, after the payment of said dividends, shall be credited to, and, at the expiration of the policies, divided among the insured, and the remaining one fourth shall be invested and be a reserve for the security of the insured; but when, from time to time, the reserve shall exceed five per cent. on the amount insured, the whole of said net profit in excess of said reserve of five per cent. shall, after the payment of said dividends, be divided among the insured at the expiration of their policies.

The guarantee capital shall be applied to the payment of losses only when the other cash funds have been exhausted; and if the guarantee capital shall at any time be reduced, it shall be replaced from the first accumulation of the reserve, or the directors may, at their discretion, replace the whole, or any part of it, by assessments upon the contingent funds in the possession of the company at the time of said reduction.

Shareholders and policy-holders in corporations referred to in this section shall be subject to the same provisions of law in voting at all meetings of such corporations as apply respectively to shareholders in joint-stock companies and policy-holders in purely mutual companies, and the directors may be elected from the stockholders or policy-holders, not less than one half being from the holders of stock. Such companies may insure property located in any part of the United States, and for its full value, and shall be subject to the provisions of chapter two hundred and eighty-three of the acts of the year eighteen hundred and sixty-five.

SECT. 12. The holders of shares in the permanent fund of any mutual marine, or mutual fire or marine insurance company, shall be entitled to a semi-annual dividend of not exceeding six per cent., and the makers of the promissory notes constituting any part of such fund shall be entitled to a semi-annual dividend not exceeding two and one half per cent. of the amount of such notes, if the net profits and income of the company, after providing for all expenses, losses, and liabilities then existing, including a sum sufficient to reinsure all outstanding risks, as provided by the laws of the Commonwealth, are sufficient to pay the same; and if any dividends are less than those amounts respectively, the same shall be made up when such net profits and income become sufficient therefor.

The directors may declare, each year, a dividend of the remainder of such net profits and income on the premiums received on risks terminated during the year, and issue certificates therefor, as provided in the general laws relating to mutual marine or mutual fire and marine insurance companies: *provided*, that no such certificate shall be redeemed until the accumulation of net profits exceed the sum of five hundred thousand dollars, and no certificates shall be redeemed until the directors so determine.

The shareholders in corporations referred to in this section shall be the members of the company, and subject to the same provisions of law in voting at all meetings of such corporations as apply to shareholders in joint-stock companies. All such companies shall be subject to the provisions of chapter two hundred and eighty-three of the acts of the year eighteen hundred and sixty-five.

SECT. 13. Any joint-stock insurance company organized under the provisions of this act may, at a meeting called for the purpose, increase the amount of its capital stock, and the number of shares therein, and, within thirty days after the payment or collection of the last instalment of such increase, shall present to the insurance commissioner a certificate setting forth the amount of such increase, and the fact of such payment, signed and sworn to by the president, secretary, and a majority of the directors of such corporation. The insurance commissioner shall examine the certificate, and ascertain the character of the investments of such increase; and, if the same conforms to law, shall endorse his approval thereof, and such certificate shall then be filed with the secretary of the Commonwealth, and thereupon the company shall be authorized to transact business upon the capital so increased, and the insurance commissioner shall issue his certificate to that effect; and any mutual insurance company with a guarantee capital may, within the limits authorized by this act, increase its capital in the same manner as a joint stock insurance company.

SECT. 14. The fees to be paid for filing and recording the certificates required by sections nine and thirteen, to be filed with the secretary of the Commonwealth, shall be as follows:

For the certificate required by section nine, twenty-five dollars.

For the certificate required by section thirteen, five dollars.

SECT. 15. Corporations organized under the provisions of this act may hold real estate for the purposes of their business, to an amount not exceeding twenty-five per cent. of their cash assets.

SECT. 16. No insurance corporation or association of any other State or country shall be hereafter admitted to do business in this State, unless it has at least the amount of unimpaired capital stock or funds required of like corporations or associations hereafter organized in this State, located in the city of Boston; and the provisions of this section, relating to capital stock or funds, shall be held applicable to all insurance corporations or associations of any other State or country doing business in this State, after the first day of January, eighteen hundred and seventy-four.

SECT. 17. No joint-stock insurance company organized under the laws of this Commonwealth, and doing the business of insurance under such organization, shall declare cash dividends exceeding in amount six per cent. semi-annually on their capital stock; but any such company may issue *pro rata* to its stockholders certificates of such portion of its profits and income as the directors may from time to time determine, not including therein any portion of the premium money of risks not terminated, and after providing for all expenses, losses, and liabilities then incurred; and the capital stock of such company shall be increased by the amount of the certificates of stock so issued; and whenever any increase of capital shall be made by any insurance company under the provisions of this act, a certificate thereof shall be filed with the insurance commissioner, whose duty it shall be to certify to the amount of the capital stock of the company so increased, in like manner as by law is provided in case of the organization of joint-stock insurance companies.

SECT. 18. The mayor and aldermen of the several cities, and the selectmen of towns having more than four thousand inhabitants, shall, before the first day of October, in the year eighteen hundred and seventy-three, divide their respective cities and towns into fire-insurance districts, and, immediately thereafter, file plans and specifications thereof with the insurance commissioner, and the same shall be subject to his approval; and if he disapprove the same, the mayor and aldermen or selectmen shall forthwith redistrict such city or town in conformity to his requirement. And no company or association transacting the business of fire insurance in this Commonwealth shall, after said first day of October, take or have at risk on property other than dwelling-houses, farm buildings, and their contents, in any town or such fire-insurance district of a city or town therein, an amount exceeding its net assets available for the payment of losses in Massachusetts; and in computing the assets of such company or association insuring property upon the mutual principle, its premium notes shall be included. When, from any cause, the net assets, as aforesaid, of any such company or association shall be reduced to a sum less than the amount taken or held at risk in any town or any such fire-insurance district, as provided in this section, such company or association shall forthwith either cancel or return to the holder the unearned portion of the premium upon policies upon property in such territory, to an amount equal to the difference between the net assets and the amount taken or held at risk, as aforesaid, or effect reinsurance upon such property for a like sum; and no such cancellation shall take place except after notice to the holder of the policy. Every such company or association shall, annually, on or before the fifteenth day of January, return to the insurance commissioner a sworn statement of the amount taken or held at risk in each town or fire-insurance district of a city in this Commonwealth, on the thirty-first day of December next preceding. The insurance commissioner may, whenever he deems expedient, require of said companies or associations such a statement, or any part thereof; he may also require such other information, and adopt such rules and regulations, as he may deem proper and necessary to procure reliable information upon this subject. For every policy issued in violation of the provisions of this section, by an insurance company incorporated under the laws of this Commonwealth, the president and secretary thereof shall, severally, upon conviction, be punished by a fine of fifty dollars. Any agent of company or association not incorporated under the laws of this Commonwealth, but duly authorized to transact business therein, shall, upon conviction, be punished by a fine of fifty dollars for each policy issued in violation of the provisions of this section, and upon a second conviction, his certificate of agency or license shall be revoked by the insurance commissioner.

SECT. 19. Any existing mutual fire insurance company, at a meeting specially called for that purpose, may, by a major vote of the policy-holders present and voting thereon, acquire a guarantee capital, as hereinbefore provided for mutual fire insurance companies with a guarantee capital; and, within thirty days after the payment or collection of the last instalment of the subscription to such guarantee capital, shall present to the insurance commissioner a certificate setting forth the fact of such vote and of such payment, signed and sworn to by the president, secretary, and a majority of the directors of such company. The insurance commissioner shall examine the certificate, and ascertain the character of the investments of said capital; and, if the same conforms to law, shall endorse his approval thereof, and such certificate shall then be filed with the secretary of the Commonwealth, and thereupon such company shall be authorized and required to transact business as a mutual fire insurance company with a guarantee capital under this act, and the insurance commissioner shall issue his certificate to that effect.

Sect. 20. If any corporation organized under this act does not commence to issue policies within one year after the date of the certificate of its organization, its corporate powers and existence shall cease.

Sect. 21. The provisions of this act, and the franchises, rights, powers, privileges, duties, and liabilities of insurance companies organized under this or any other general act, may be altered, amended, or repealed, and the legislature may annul or dissolve any such corporation.

Sect. 22. This act shall take effect upon its passage.
Approved, December 18, 1872.

CHAPTER 371.

AN ACT

In addition to an act to provide for the regulation and inspection of buildings, the more effectual prevention of fire, and the better preservation of life and property in Boston.

Be it enacted by the Senate and House of Representatives, in General Court assembled, and by the authority of the same, as follows :

Section 1. Section three of chapter two hundred and sixty of the acts of the year eighteen hundred and seventy-two is amended, so that the same shall read as follows :

Buildings other than dwelling-houses shall have walls of the following thickness :

For buildings in which the walls do not exceed thirty-five feet in height, the foundation walls shall be laid of block stone in horizontal courses not less than twenty-four inches thick, the external walls shall not be less than sixteen inches thick to the top of the upper floor, and not less than twelve inches thick for the remaining height.

For buildings in which the walls exceed thirty-five feet in height, the foundation walls shall be laid of block stone in horizontal courses not less than twenty-eight inches thick, the external walls not less than twenty inches thick to the top of the third floor, and not less than sixteen inches thick for the remaining height.

All party walls shall not be less than twenty inches thick to the top of the second floor above the street, and not less than sixteen inches thick to the under side of the roof-boards, and not less than twelve inches thick for the remaining height.

In all buildings over twenty-five feet in width, not having either brick partition walls, or girders supported by columns running from front to rear, the external walls shall be increased four inches in thickness, for every additional twenty-five feet in the width of said building.

The amount of materials above specified for external walls may be used either in piers or buttresses: *provided*, the external walls between the said piers or buttresses shall in no case be less than sixteen inches thick.

The bottom course for all foundation walls resting upon the ground shall be at least twelve inches wider than the thickness above given for the foundation walls.

SECT. 2. Section twenty-one of chapter two hundred and eighty of the acts of the year eighteen hundred and seventy-one is amended, so that the same shall read as follows:

For dwelling-houses with walls not exceeding thirty-five feet in height, foundation walls, laid with block stone in horizontal courses, or in brick laid in cement, shall be not less than sixteen inches thick, and external and party walls of brick shall be not less than twelve inches thick for the entire height.

For dwelling-houses with walls exceeding thirty-five and not exceeding fifty-five feet in height, foundation walls laid with block stone in horizontal courses shall be not less than eighteen inches thick; if of brick, the foundation walls shall be sixteen inches thick, and laid in cement. External brick walls shall be not less than twelve inches thick; party walls of brick shall not be less than twelve inches thick for the entire height.

For dwelling-houses with walls exceeding fifty-five feet in height, foundation walls, laid with block stone in horizontal courses, or brick laid in cement, shall be not less than twenty inches thick. External and party brick walls shall be not less than twelve inches thick for the entire height.

The thickness of foundation walls laid with irregular rubble-work shall be one fourth greater than the thickness given for block stone walls.

SECT. 3. The height of every external or party wall, as referred to in this act, or in the act of which this act is an amendment, or in any act in amendment thereof, shall be measured from the level of the sidewalk to its highest point.

SECT. 4. The external walls of buildings intended to be used for stables or for workshops of a light character may be built of a less thickness than hereinbefore specified : *provided*, that any such building shall not exceed thirty feet in height to its highest point, and forty feet in length or width, and that the said walls shall in no case be less than twelve inches thick. Vaulted party walls may be used instead of solid walls. They shall be built at least twenty inches thick from the foundation walls to the under side of the roof boarding. Said walls shall be constructed of two outer walls of equal thickness, with an air-space between them of four inches, and tied together perpendicularly with continuous withes of hard-burned brick of good quality, which shall not be more than three feet apart. The air-space shall be smoothly plastered.

SECT. 5. In every brick wall, every ninth course of brick shall be a heading course, except in walls built with some bond in which as much as every ninth course is a heading course, and except where walls are faced with face brick, in which case every ninth course shall be bonded into the backing by cutting the course of the faced brick and putting in diagonal headers behind the same, or by splitting face brick in half, and backing the same by a continuous row of headers. In all walls which are faced with thin ashlar, anchored to the backing, or in which the ashlar has not either alternate headers and stretchers in each course, or alternate heading and stretching courses, the backing of brick shall not be less than twelve inches thick, and shall not be built to a greater height than prescribed for twelve-inch walls. All heading courses shall be good, hard, perfect brick. The backing in all walls, of whatever material it may be composed, shall be of such thickness as to make all walls, the facing of which is less than four inches thick, independent of the facing, conform, as to thickness, with the requirements of sections one and two of this act.

SECT. 6. Every building hereafter erected, more than thirty feet in width, except churches, theatres, railroad-station buildings, and other public buildings, shall have one or more brick or stone partition walls running from front to rear, and carried up to a height not less than the top of the second-story floor joists; said wall or walls may be four inches less in thickness than is called for by the provisions relating to the thickness of walls; these walls shall be so located that the space between any two of the floor-bearing walls of the building shall not be over twenty-five feet. Iron or wooden girders, supported upon iron or wooden columns, may be substituted in place of partition walls, and shall be made of sufficient strength to bear safely the weight which they are intended to support, in addition to the weight of material employed in their construction, and shall have a footing course and foundation wall not less than eighteen inches in thickness, or piers of a size and strength equivalent thereto.

SECT. 7. It shall not be lawful to erect, construct, or build any rear, front, party, division or partition wall, upon wooden girders, rafters or lintels, or to support any such wall by any wooden support whatever; but all such supports shall be of iron, brick, or stone, and of sufficient size and strength to support the superstructure. All lintels used to support walls or other weights over openings shall be of sufficient strength and bearing to carry the superimposed weight, and shall, when supported at the end by brick walls or piers, rest upon an iron plate at least two inches thick, the full size of the bearing.

No floor-beams shall be supported wholly upon any wood partition, but every beam (except headers and tail beams) shall rest, at one end, not less than four inches in the wall, or upon a girder, as authorized by this act. And every trimmer or header more than four feet long, used in any building except a dwelling, shall be hung in stirrup-irons, of suitable thickness for the size of the timbers. No timber shall be used in any wall of any building where stone, brick, or iron is commonly used, except bond timbers and lintels, as hereinbefore provided for, or as may be approved of by the inspector of buildings; and no bond timber in any wall shall in width and thickness exceed that of a course of brick. No bond timber shall be more than three feet in length, and such bond timbers shall be laid not less than eighteen inches apart, parallel to each other, and there shall be eight inches of brick or mason-work between the ends of the same. The butts or ends of all floor beams and rafters entering a brick wall shall be cut on a splay of three inches in their width.

All main partitions, supporting in any manner the floor beams or rafters, shall be placed directly over each other, and shall rest on a wall, girder, or hard pine capping, and shall head and foot against each other as far as practicable.

SECT. 8. All piers shall be built of good, hard, well-burnt brick, and laid in clear cement, and all bricks used in piers shall be of the hardest quality, and be well wet when laid; and the walls and piers under all compound, cast-iron, or wooden girders, iron or other columns, shall have a bond iron at least two inches in thickness, and if in a wall, at least two feet in length, running through the wall, and if in a pier, the full size of the thickness thereof, every thirty inches in height from the bottom, whether said pier is in the wall or not, and shall have a cap of iron, at least two inches in thickness, satisfactory to the inspector of buildings, by the whole size of the pier, if in a pier, and if in a wall, it shall be at least two feet in length by the thickness of the wall, and of the thicknesses above specified. All brick walls in buildings other than dwelling-houses shall be corbelled to receive floor timbers, and such timbers shall be supported thereby. In case vaulted walls are used, the corbelling to receive floor timbers may be dispensed with. In any case where any iron or other column rests on any wall or pier built entirely of stone or brick, the said column shall be set on an iron plate at least two inches thick, of the size of said pier. When any outer wall is supported in whole or in part by columns or pillars, the depth of base and head of such columns or pillars shall be equal to the required thickness of the wall thereby supported.

SECT. 9. In all calculations for the strength of materials to be used in any building, the proportion between the safe weight and the breaking weight shall be as one to three for all beams, girders, and other pieces subjected to a cross strain, and as one to six for all posts, columns, and other vertical supports, and for all tie-rods, tie-beams, and other pieces subjected to a tensile strain; and the requisite dimensions of each piece of material is to be ascertained by computation by the rules given by the best authorities, using for constants in the rules only such numbers as have been deduced from experiments on materials of like kind with that proposed to be used.

SECT. 10. In no case shall the side, end, or party wall of any building be carried up in advance of the rear walls. The front, rear, side, end, and party walls of any building hereafter to be erected shall be anchored to each other every ten feet in their height, by tie-anchors, made of at least one and a quarter inch by three eighths of an inch, wrought iron. The said anchors shall be built into the side or party walls not less than thirty-six inches, and into the front and rear walls at least one half the thickness of the front and rear walls, so as to secure the front and rear walls to the side, end, or party walls.

The side, end, or party walls shall be anchored at each tier of beams, at intervals of not more than ten feet apart, with good strong wrought-iron anchors, at least one half inch by one and one half inch; well built into the side walls, and fastened to the top of the beams, and where the beams are supported by girders, the ends of the beams resting on the girder shall be butted together, end to end, and strapped by wrought iron straps, or tie-irons, at the same distances apart, and on the same beams as the wall-anchors, and shall be well fastened.

All mortar shall be of the best quality for the purpose for which it is applied.

SECT. 11. All party walls shall be carried up to a height of not less than two and one half feet above the roof covering, with the full thickness of the party wall, and shall be coped with stone or iron, securely fastened. And where there is a flat, hip, or pitch roof, the party wall shall be carried up to a height of not less than two and one half feet above the roof covering, at every part of said roof, and shall be corbelled at least twelve inches, or to the outer edge of all projections on the front or rear walls of the building. And where the roof is of the kind known as Mansard, or French, or of any style excepting as above specified, unless the same is constructed of fire-proof materials throughout, the party wall shall be carried up to a height of not less than two and one half feet above the flat or upper slope of said roof, and shall extend through the lower slope, at least eighteen inches distant from the parallel with the roof covering, and be corbelled out at least twelve inches, or to the outer edge of all projections, and shall be coped with stone or iron: *provided*, that if a gutter-stone of suitable dimensions and properly balanced shall be inserted, it shall be equivalent to corbelling.

All roof or floor timbers entering the same party wall from opposite sides shall have at least four inches solid brickwork between the ends of said timbers.

SECT. 12. All stores or storehouses that may hereafter be built in said city, which are more than forty-five feet in height above the curb level, shall have doors, blinds, or shutters, made of fire-proof metal, on every window and entrance where the same do not open on a street. When in any such building the shutters, blinds, or doors cannot be put on the outside of such door or window, they shall be put on the inside, and if placed on the inside shall be hung upon an iron frame independent of the woodwork of the window-frame or door; and every such door, blind, or shutter shall be closed upon the completion of the business of each day by the occupant having the use or control of the same; and all fire-proof shutters or blinds, that now are or may hereafter be put upon the front or sides of any building on the street fronts, must be so constructed that they can be closed and opened from the outside above the first story.

SECT. 13. All buildings hereafter erected, to be used for railroad stations, public assemblies, schoolhouses, hotels, lodging or tenement-houses, and manufactories, where there are to be more than twenty-five persons resident, assembled, or employed, above the first floor, shall be provided with staircases of, and enclosed with, non-combustible materials, and of a width to be approved by the inspector of buildings, and provided with doors opening outward.

SECT. 14. Any building already erected, or that may hereafter be erected, in which operatives are employed in any of the stories above the second story, shall be provided with such fire-escapes as shall be directed and approved by the inspector of buildings. And the owner or owners of any buildings upon which any fire-escapes may now be, or may hereafter be erected, shall keep the same in good repair and well painted. And no person shall at any time place any incumbrance of any kind whatever upon any said fire-escapes now erected, or that may hereafter be erected in said city.

Sect. 15. All buildings in the city of Boston hereafter to be built shall have scuttle-frames and covers, or bulkheads and doors on the roof, made of or covered with fire-proof material, and all scuttles shall have stationary ladders leading to the same, and all such scuttles or ladders shall be kept so as to be ready for use at all times, and all scuttles shall not be less in size than two by three feet; and if a bulkhead is used or substituted in any building in place of a scuttle, it shall have stairs with a sufficient guard or hand-rail leading to the roof; and in case the building shall be a tenement-house, the door in the bulkhead, or any scuttle, shall at no time be locked, but may be fastened on the inside by movable hooks or locks.

Sect. 16. No smoke-pipe in any building with wooden or combustible floors and ceilings shall hereafter enter any flue unless the said pipe where it enters the flue shall be at least twelve inches from either the floors or ceilings; and in all cases where smoke-pipes pass through stud or wooden partitions of any kind, whether the same be plastered or not, they shall be guarded by a soapstone ring, not less than four inches in thickness, and extend through the partition. In all cases where hot water, steam, hot-air, or other furnaces are used, the furnace smoke-pipe must be kept at least two feet below the beams or ceiling above the same, unless said beams or ceiling shall be properly protected by a shield or tin plate suspended at least one inch below said beams or ceiling above said smoke-pipe; and the top of all furnaces set in brick must be covered with brick, supported by iron bars and so constructed as to be perfectly tight; said covering to be in addition to and not less than six inches from the ordinary covering to the hot-air chamber. If, however, there is not height enough to build the furnace top to at least four inches below the floor-beams or ceilings, then the floor-beams must be trimmed around the furnace, and said covering and the trimmers and headers must be at least four inches from the same. The top of every portable furnace not set in brick shall be kept at least one foot below the beams or ceiling with a shield of tin plate, made tight, and suspended not less than one inch below the said beams or ceilings, and extended one foot beyond the top of the furnace on all sides. All hot-air registers hereafter placed in the floor of any building shall be set in soapstone borders not less than two inches in width. All soapstone borders to be firmly set in plaster of Paris or gauged mortar. All floor register-boxes to be made of tin plate, with a flange on the top to fit the groove in the soapstone, the register to rest upon the same. There shall also be an open space of one inch on all sides of the register-box, extending from the under side of the ceiling, below the register, to the soapstone in the floor; the outside of said space to be covered with a casing of tin plate, made tight on all sides, to extend from the under side of the aforesaid ceiling up to and turn under the said soapstone. Registers of fifteen by twenty-five inches, or more, shall have a space of two inches. No woodwork shall be placed at a less distance than one inch from any tin or other metal flue or flues, pipe or pipes, used or intended to be used to convey heated air in any building, unless protected by a soapstone or earthen ring or tube, or a metal casing so constructed as to permit free circulation of air around said pipes or flues. In all cases where hot-water, steam, hot-air, or other furnaces or ranges, are hereafter placed, or their location changed, in any building, due notice shall first be given to the inspector of buildings, by the person or persons placing said furnace or ranges in said building.

In all cases where ranges or boilers are set, the outside of the flue to the same shall be plastered on the outside directly upon the bricks up to the ceiling of the room.

SECT. 17. If any chimney, flue, or heating apparatus on any premises in the city of Boston shall, in the opinion of the inspector of buildings, be dangerous or unsafe by reason of endangering the premises by fire or otherwise, the inspector shall at once notify, in writing, the owner, agent, or other party having an interest in said premises, and shall require him to make the same safe; and upon neglect of said person so notified to comply with the provisions of said notice, for a period of twenty-four hours after the service of said notice upon him, he shall at once become liable to a penalty of not less than twenty, nor more than fifty dollars, for every day's continuance of said unsafe structure.

SECT. 18. All boiler or engine-rooms hereafter constructed in any building other than dwelling-houses shall be constructed of brick and iron, and shall be so arranged that all openings between the said boiler or engine-room, and other parts of the building in which it is placed, shall be closed by iron or metal covered doors, which shall be securely closed at the close of each day.

Upon a license being granted by the mayor and board of aldermen of the city of Boston for the erection of a steam-boiler, engine, or furnace for melting glass, iron, or other metal, in any building in the said city, the person or persons receiving said license shall, before setting, erecting, or placing said boiler, engine, or furnace, file an application for a permit therefor, with the inspector of buildings, who shall prescribe such regulations for the setting or placing thereof as the public safety may require; and no person or persons shall erect, set, or place any boiler, engine, furnace, or oven without a permit from said inspector.

All flues for ranges, boilers, furnaces, and ovens, shall be of brickwork, eight inches in thickness, to a height of twenty-five feet above such ranges, boilers, furnaces, or ovens.

SECT. 19. No Mansard or other roof shall be constructed more than one story in height, nor more than twenty feet in height from the upper floor of the building upon which it is placed, to the highest part of said roof, unless the same is constructed of fire-proof material throughout. No bay window shall be constructed of wood, which shall extend more than three feet above the second story from the street.

All the exterior parts of any building or buildings hereafter erected, which are more than forty-five feet above the level of the sidewalk, shall be made of or covered with non-combustible material, to be approved by the inspector of buildings. All fire-proof cornices shall be well secured to the walls with iron anchors, independent of any woodwork; and in all cases the walls shall be carried up to the planking of the roof, and where the cornice projects above the roof, the wall shall be carried up to the top of the cornices, and all exterior wooden cornices that shall hereafter require to be replaced shall be constructed of some non-combustible material, as required for new buildings; and all exterior wooden cornices or gutters that may hereafter be damaged by fire shall be taken down, and, if replaced, shall be constructed of fire-proof material.

All buildings hereafter erected shall be kept provided with proper metallic leaders for conducting the water from the roof to the ground, sewer, or street gutter, in such manner as shall protect the walls and foundations from damage; and in no case shall the water from the said leaders be allowed to flow upon the sidewalk, but shall be conducted by drain-pipe, or pipes, to the street gutter or sewer.

SECT. 20. All buildings hereafter erected, the eaves of which exceed sixty feet in height above the level of the sidewalk, shall have the roofs thereof constructed in a fire-proof manner, as hereinafter specified; but the total height of such buildings, exclusive of chimneys and party walls, shall not exceed seventy-five feet.

All joists, beams, rafters, purlins, jack rafters, plates, struts, ties, arches, shall be made of cast or wrought iron, or some other metal, stone, brick, cement, mortar, or other incombustible material, and covered with corrugated iron, sheet or cast iron, tin, copper, zinc, or other metal, or slate, stone, brick, cement, mortar, or other incombustible material.

All structures or projections above or outside of the roof, such as domes, cupolas, pavilions, towers, spires, pinnacles, buttresses, lanterns, louvres, luthern and dormer windows, skylights, scuttles, ventilators, cornices, gutters, shall be made, constructed, framed, and covered with cast or wrought iron, tin, copper, zinc, or other metal, or stone, slate, brick, cement, or mortar, or other incombustible material.

SECT. 21. No building already erected, or hereafter to be built in said city, shall be raised or built upon in such manner that, were such building wholly built or constructed after the passage of this act, it would be in violation of any of the provisions of this act. And before any building built of stone, brick, or iron, or any wooden building with or without a brick front, in any part of said city, shall be enlarged, raised, altered, or built upon, the same shall be first examined by the said inspector, to ascertain if the building or buildings, or either of them, are in a good and safe condition to be enlarged, raised, altered, or built upon; and no such buildings as aforesaid shall be enlarged, raised, altered, or built upon until after such examination and decision; and the decision of said inspector, under such examination, shall be final and conclusive in the premises, except as hereinafter provided, and shall be made without delay.

SECT. 22. The inspector of buildings shall have full power to pass upon any question arising under the provisions of this act, relative to the manner of construction, or materials to be used in the erection, alteration, or repair of any building in the city of Boston, and he may require that plans of the proposed erection, alterations, or repairs, shall be submitted for inspection before issuing his permit : *provided*, however, that should any question arise between the inspector of buildings and the owner or architect of any building, or should the owner or architect object to any order or decision of said inspector, the matter shall be referred to a committee of three persons, who shall be either architects or master-builders, one to be chosen by the inspector of buildings, one by the owner or other interested party, and these two shall choose a third; and the decision of these referees, submitted in writing, shall be final and conclusive in the premises.

PENALTIES.

SECT. 23. If any person or persons, whether owner or owners, contractor or contractors, builder or builders, shall begin to erect, construct, build, or alter any building or structure, within the city of Boston, without first obtaining a permit from the inspector of buildings of said city, such person or persons shall forfeit and pay the sum of not less than one hundred dollars, nor more than one thousand dollars, for each and every such offence; and if any person or persons, as aforesaid, shall proceed to complete any building or structure in the city of Boston, without having the same inspected as by law required, or shall violate any or either of the provisions of this act, or the act of which this act is an amendment, or of any other act in amendment thereof, for the violation of which no other penalties are therein or hereinbefore provided, he or they shall forfeit and pay not less than one hundred dollars, and not more than one thousand dollars, for each and every such violation, and the further sum of one hundred dollars for each and every week that he or they shall maintain any building or structure in violation of any provision of this act, or of the act of which this act is an amendment, or of any other act in amendment thereof. All penalties under this act shall be recoverable by the city of Boston in an action of tort. If any person or persons, whether owner or owners, contractor or contractors, builder or builders, shall erect or alter any building or structure in the city of Boston, in violation of any or either of the provisions of this act, or of the act of which this act is an amendment, or of any amendment thereof, it shall be lawful for the supreme judicial court, or any justice thereof, either in term-time or in vacation, to issue forthwith an injunction, restraining such person or persons from further progress in said work until the facts of the case shall have been investigated and determined; and if it shall appear to said court, or to any justice thereof, upon such investigation, that such building or structure does not in all respects conform to the provisions of this act, and of the act of which this act is an amendment, and of all amendments thereof, said court or justice shall issue an injunction to restrain the continuance of the work upon such building or structure, and shall order the removal, within a time to be fixed by said court or justice, of so much of said building or structure as may be decreed by said court or justice to be in violation of the provisions of this act, or of the act of which this act is an amendment, or of any act in amendment thereof.

SECT. 24. The provisions of this act shall not apply to the passenger stations of the Boston and Lowell, and Boston and Providence Railroad corporations, now in process of erection in the city of Boston; but such precautions shall be provided for protection against, and for the extinguishment of, fire, under the penalties of this act, as the inspector of public buildings shall require.

Sect. 25. The inspector and assistant inspector of the department for the survey and inspection of buildings in the city of Boston, shall be able and experienced architects, builders, or mechanics, competent to perform all the duties of the office to which they are appointed, and such inspectors shall not be employed or engaged in any other vocation, or be interested in any contract or contracts for building or for furnishing materials.

Sect. 26. This act shall take effect upon its passage.

Approved, December 14, 1872.

www.ingramcontent.com/pod-product-compliance
Lightning Source LLC
Chambersburg PA
CBHW030405170426
43202CB00010B/1495